MW00607714

A Clinician's Guide to

Gaslighting

80+ worksheets and exercises

for detection, intervention, and healing from emotional abuse

STEPHANIE MOULTON SARKIS, PhD, NCC, DCMHS, LMHC

A CLINICIAN'S GUIDE TO GASLIGHTING
Copyright © 2024 by Sarkis Media LLC

Published by
PESI Publishing, Inc.
3839 White Ave
Eau Claire, WI 54703

Cover and interior design by Emily Dyer
Editing by Jenessa Jackson, PhD

ISBN 9781683737513 (print)
ISBN 9781683737520 (ePUB)
ISBN 9781683737537 (ePDF)

All rights reserved.
Printed in the United States of America.

PESI Publishing
pesipublishing.com

Table of Contents

Introduction

Gaslighting is an insidious form of emotional abuse where survivors are made to question their reality. Not only does gaslighting cause immense damage to clients' psychological and physical health, but it can be one of the first signs of escalating abuse in a relationship. Using the activities and exercises in this workbook, you can help clients identify and extract themselves from unbearable suffering perpetrated by narcissists and sociopaths.

I've been a licensed mental health counselor for over 20 years, and when I first began practicing, my primary areas of expertise were attention-deficit/hyperactivity disorder (ADHD) and anxiety. Over the years, I noticed that an increasing number of clients were saying that they felt they were being gaslit in their relationships. They often described behaviors where their partners told them they couldn't be trusted or were fabricating events due to their disorders. When a client has any medical condition, such as ADHD, or has suffered a loss, such as the death of a spouse, they are more vulnerable to a gaslighter or narcissist preying upon them. The gaslighter will use the client's medical conditions against them to "prove" that their version of reality is wrong and convince them that the gaslighter has the "correct" version of reality.

During this time, I knew emotional abuse was a form of domestic violence, as did other clinicians in the field, but many in society still viewed it as not a "real" thing. In many cases today, gaslighting and other forms of emotional abuse are still not considered domestic violence. Suppose you've had a client apply for a restraining order from the courts. In that case, you are well aware that emotional abuse is often not considered "dangerous" enough for your client to receive legal protection. In contrast, a client experiencing physical abuse is much more likely to be approved for an injunction. Consider that in 2018, the U.S. Department of Justice (DOJ) changed the definition of domestic violence on its website to only include physical abuse, thereby eliminating sexual, emotional, psychological, and financial abuse from the description. Since 2021, the DOJ website has been updated to reflect that domestic violence includes all forms of abuse, but we still have a long way to go to protect those who have experienced these "other" forms of domestic violence.

Why I Wrote This Workbook

Given my time with clients disclosing their experiences with gaslighting, I wrote an article for *Psychology Today* in 2017 called "11 Red Flags of Gaslighting in a Relationship." The article went viral and has over 20 million hits as of this printing. That article and its ensuing response led me to write my bestselling book *Gaslighting: Recognize Manipulative and Emotionally Abusive People—and Break Free*. While the audience of *Gaslighting* is primarily those who have experienced it, the good people at PESI saw the need for a gaslighting workbook for clinicians.

As a therapist, you are likely one of the very few people to whom survivors have disclosed gaslighting abuse. That's because gaslighters isolate and control their victims by making them dependent on the gaslighter's version of reality. Clients are told that their friends and family will think they are crazy and that no one will believe them if they report the abuse. When a gaslighter fully dismantles a client's boundaries, they are systematically distanced from their support network. Often, you may be the client's only outside contact and the only constant in their lives.

Due to the insidious nature of gaslighting, you may need additional information on how to identify it and help clients heal. Survivors themselves may not have come to terms with the fact that they were subjected to abuse. Many survivors blame themselves for the gaslighter's behaviors—they've been told they are the problem in the relationship, which traps them in a web of manipulation and control. Remember that emotional abuse still has the stigma of being an invisible form of abuse, even though it can cause more trauma than physical abuse (Strathearn et al., 2020). By understanding the behavior patterns of gaslighters, you can better identify this form of emotional abuse and provide clients with the safe, trusting, and supportive environment they need to heal and rebuild their lives. Without understanding this pattern of behavior, you could fail to see the trauma and abuse these clients have endured, mirroring the gaslighting they've already experienced and leading to further trauma.

What Is in This Workbook

This workbook provides resources for you and your clients so you can identify, validate, and treat the lasting effects of gaslighting and other forms of emotional abuse. Inside, you will find:

- Detailed definitions and checklists for gaslighting, emotional abuse, and other forms of domestic violence

- Guidance for differentiating between gaslighting and poor communication in a relationship

- Delineation of behaviors frequently seen in toxic relationships, such as love bombing, hoovering, and the idealization-devaluation-discarding cycle

- Discussions of the origins and causes of gaslighting behavior

- A breakdown of the connection between cluster B personality disorders and gaslighting

- Psychoeducation and tools for clients who grew up with gaslighting or narcissistic parents

- Strategies for identifying and responding to gaslighting and emotional abuse in organizations

- Detailed steps for establishing (and maintaining) no-contact and low-contact with gaslighters and narcissists

- Tools to help clients rebuild healthy boundaries

- A safety plan for clients who are planning on leaving an abusive relationship

- Ways to help clients reconnect with trusted family and friends

- Options for clients who are coparenting with a gaslighter or narcissist

- Information on preventing and treating vicarious trauma in yourself

- Coping skills and self-care practices to support you as well as your clients

- And more!

Since clients may not be aware of the extent of the emotional abuse they have experienced or may be deep in denial as a form of self-protection, this workbook addresses how to meet clients where they are when discussing gaslighting and abuse. Be aware when you are working harder than your client and when you may envision a path to healing for your client that they are not yet ready to pursue. It is important to let clients work at their own pace. You don't have to use the activities and worksheets sequentially. It is perfectly okay to jump around and find material that works best for you and the client at any stage of treatment.

How to Use This Workbook

When making your way through this workbook, I encourage you to assign many of these activities and worksheets for homework, as this is a simple yet effective way to continue the healing process when your client is not in session. Your clients may feel isolated between sessions, especially if they are caught in (or have recently ended) an abusive relationship. Since gaslighters work to separate victims from their friends and family members, having a link between your client and a future session can help provide them with a sense of safety and continuity.

The handouts and worksheets are designed to be stand-alone and simple to use, meaning your client will not need any extra tools, information, or resources to complete them successfully. Review the exercises with your client before assigning them as homework and, at the next session, discuss any potential difficulties they had in completing the assignment. The activities should provide enough of a challenge to motivate your client but not so much that it causes them insurmountable frustration. Let your client know that growth can sometimes be uncomfortable and even painful. If a client does not complete an assignment, avoid asking why. Instead, ask them what parts of the assignment were challenging and explore what life circumstances may have led them not to complete it. The reality is that they may not have had time alone. As the therapist, it is appropriate for you to be concerned yet supportive.

As you've heard in clinical practice, you get out of it what you put into it. You can dive deep into this workbook or skim it as needed. However, I encourage you to read it through from cover to cover, especially if you have not yet had much training or experience in working with survivors of gaslighting. You can then decide which exercises are appropriate for particular clients. I have also included therapist worksheets to increase your understanding of this pathological form of emotional abuse.

I know for others among you, the world of gaslighting will be all too familiar. You may have experienced gaslighting and narcissistic abuse in your family of origin or other relationships, or you may have specialized training in treating survivors of domestic violence and know the signs of gaslighting well. Either way, you may be relieved that gaslighting is being discussed more openly in the mental health community and the world at large. Whether you are working with clients who already identify as survivors of gaslighting and narcissistic abuse or those who show signs that they may be experiencing it, the tools in this workbook can help them break free from the cycle of manipulation and find the healing they deserve.

CHAPTER 1

Basics of Gaslighting

While the term *gaslighting* has been used for decades to describe a form of emotional abuse, the word wasn't commonly used until the mid-2010s. During this time, the term increased in popularity as there was a societal shift toward correctly classifying emotional abuse as a form of violence. Not only is gaslighting a very prevalent phenomenon, but it is a gateway to other forms of abuse. For example, in relationships where there is intimate partner violence, 80 percent of survivors report having experienced emotional abuse, including gaslighting (Karakurt & Silver, 2013). Individuals in these abusive relationships are made to question their reality and are told that what they saw or heard didn't happen, even if they have proof.

If a client has a mental health issue, the gaslighter will also weaponize it against them. For example, the gaslighter might hide items of great sentimental or monetary value and tell the victim that they would have better control over their possessions if they didn't have ADHD, depression, anxiety, and so forth. The gaslighter may also claim to be very concerned about the victim's "inability" to maintain track of their possessions and ramp up this behavior by telling the victim that they should sign over control of their finances due to the supposed "lack of judgment" they have shown.

Gaslighters often learn this manipulative behavior in their family of origin and may behave this way to gain power and control or to receive an endorphin boost from successfully manipulating others (Bandelow & Wedekind, 2015). While most people experience these "feel-good" hormones when they engage in a healthy pleasurable activity, gaslighters may get this endorphin rush from victimizing others. The more social or occupational status their victim has, the greater the reward gaslighters get. Their ultimate goal is to gain power and control over a person or group of people.

In this chapter, you'll learn about the forms of domestic violence that can accompany gaslighting, the standard terms used by clinicians who specialize in gaslighting and narcissistic abuse, questions to ask your client to determine whether they are in a gaslighting relationship, and the difference between gaslighting and poor communication.

Gaslighting as a Form of Domestic Violence

Because gaslighting involves gaining control or power over another person, it is a form of emotional abuse that constitutes domestic violence. When you are working with a survivor of gaslighting or suspect that the client is being gaslit, it is vital that you learn about all the forms of domestic violence, as relationships characterized by emotional abuse are likely to consist of other forms of abuse too. Traditionally, domestic violence was thought only to include physical abuse, but abuse can take many other forms: emotional, physical, verbal, financial, sexual, and technological. The following table describes the different types of abuse that qualify as domestic violence.

Emotional	Physical	Verbal
• Gaslighting • Making threats • Playing "pranks" • Intimidating others • Openly leaving firearms around the home • Commenting on the power of firearms and other weapons in the home • Engaging in parental alienation* • Leaving someone stranded away from home • Criticizing someone's clothing by saying it is too "revealing" or "sexy"	• Blocking someone's exit • Backing someone into a corner • Slapping • Hitting • Punching • Kicking • Pinching • Hitting someone with an object • Throwing an object at someone or near them • Excessive tickling • Denying someone sleep • Inflicting pain on others or animals • Using a weapon	• Screaming or yelling • Using derogatory names • Telling children that they don't have to listen to their parent • Criticizing someone in front of others • Using non-constructive criticism • Manipulating others, particularly by using fear, obligation, and guilt • Ridiculing someone • Making threats • Using condescension • Blaming others
Financial	**Sexual**	**Technological**
• Forcing someone to quit their job • Making an adult earn an "allowance" • Engaging in human trafficking, including forced prostitution • Holding or hiding essential documents, such as passports or immigration papers • Refusing to help pay for one's children's needs • Refusing to pay bills or threatening to refuse payment	• Rape • "Punishing" someone by withholding sex • Making someone "earn" sex • Having sex with a person while they are sleeping or otherwise unconscious • Forcing someone to engage in a sexual practice they find degrading or are otherwise not interested in doing • Ridiculing someone's body or sexual performance	• Cyberstalking • Using tracking devices and cameras • Hacking into someone's email or social media account • Accessing someone's devices without explicit permission • Posting intimate photos online • Harassing and bullying others online

* For more information on parental alienation, see chapter 11.

Gaslighting Glossary

Several terms have been used to describe gaslighting behaviors. You may be familiar with some of these terms as they relate to other mental health issues (e.g., *splitting* as it is associated with borderline personality disorder). Here are their definitions within the specific context of relationships characterized by emotional abuse:

- **Gaslighting:** Keeping a victim off-kilter by making them question their reality

- **Triangulating:** Talking through a third party instead of directly to the person

- **Love bombing:** Showering the victim with extreme displays of attention and affection in order to gain control over them

- **Narcissistic supply:** A person or thing that temporarily fills the gaslighter's need for constant attention

- **Future-faking:** Making promises to lure someone back into contact

- **Double bind:** Giving a victim "choices" where they lose either way

- **Flying monkey:** A person who carries messages from a gaslighter to a victim

- **Idealization:** The initial love-bombing stage of a gaslighting relationship

- **Devaluation:** The stage of a gaslighting relationship where abuse starts (which usually follows the idealization phase)

- **Discarding:** The stage of a gaslighting relationship when the gaslighter abandons the victim (which generally follows the devaluation stage)

- **Hoovering:** Luring a victim back into contact or a relationship (which sometimes occurs after the discarding stage)

- **Splitting:** Seeing someone as all bad or all good, with no nuances

- **Fleas:** Originating from the phrase "when you lie down with dogs, you get up with fleas," this reflects the phenomenon whereby clients from a narcissistic family of origin may carry gaslighting traits into adulthood

- **Stonewalling:** Punishing someone by ignoring and refusing to communicate with them

- **Narcissistic rage:** An extreme level of anger a gaslighter displays when they don't get their way or feel that someone is "disloyal" to them

- **Mirroring:** When a gaslighter copies a victim's nonverbal behaviors and creates uncanny similarities to the victim in the early stages of a relationship

- **FOG:** Stands for fear, obligation, and guilt and reflects the many ways a gaslighter tries to manipulate their victims

The following handout will help your clients identify these gaslighting and emotionally abusive behaviors.

Gaslighting Terms

Therapists often use specific language to describe toxic relationships and to help you process your experiences. If your therapist uses any words that you are not familiar with, please let them know. Some of the more commonly used terms are also defined here:

- **Gaslighting:** When a toxic person keeps you off-kilter by making you question your sanity and reality

- **Triangulating:** When a gaslighter talks to you through a third party instead of directly going to you

- **Love bombing:** When a toxic person showers you with extreme displays of attention and affection so they can gain control over you

- **Narcissistic supply:** A person or thing that temporarily fills the gaslighter's constant need for attention

- **Future-faking:** When a gaslighter makes false promises (e.g., by love bombing or hoovering you) to lure you back into contact

- **Double bind:** When a gaslighter gives you "options" where you are damned if you do and damned if you don't

- **Flying monkey:** A person who carries messages to you from a gaslighter

- **Idealization:** The initial love-bombing phase of a toxic relationship where a gaslighter will seem to be "too good to be true" and push for commitment

- **Devaluation:** The stage of a toxic relationship where criticism and abusive behavior begin once the gaslighter knows you have been lured in by love bombing (this follows the idealization stage)

- **Discarding:** The stage of a toxic relationship where a gaslighter will abruptly leave you or use other people as narcissistic supply (this follows the devaluation stage)

- **Hoovering:** When a toxic person lures you back into contact or a relationship (this often occurs after the discarding stage)

- **Splitting:** When someone sees you as all bad or all good, meaning you are either put on a pedestal (idealization) or viewed as lower than dirt (devaluation and discarding)

- **Fleas:** Originating from the phrase "when you lie down with dogs, you get up with fleas," this reflects how someone may carry gaslighting traits into adulthood if they have been raised by a gaslighting parent

Copyright © 2024 Sarkis Media LLC, *A Clinician's Guide to Gaslighting*. All rights reserved.

- **Stonewalling:** When a gaslighter punishes you by ignoring and refusing to communicate with you

- **Narcissistic rage:** An extreme level of anger a gaslighter displays when they don't get their way or feel that you are being "disloyal" to them

- **Mirroring:** When a gaslighter copies your body language and interests to make you trust them (usually during the idealization phase)

- **FOG:** Stands for fear, obligation, and guilt and reflects the many ways a gaslighter tries to manipulate you

Copyright © 2024 Sarkis Media LLC, *A Clinician's Guide to Gaslighting.* All rights reserved.

Questions for Uncovering Gaslighting Abuse in Your Clients' Relationships

You may have clients that come in and wonder what they are "doing wrong" in their romantic relationships. They may also blame themselves for another person's pathological behavior. The following questions can help you determine whether gaslighting is a factor in your client's relationship:

1. Has your partner told you that people close to you have said bad things about you?

2. Do items of significant value or sentimentality go missing in your home without explanation?

3. Has your partner turned your children against you or undermined your parenting?

4. Has your partner ever told you that you're crazy by claiming that something you saw or heard didn't happen?

5. Did your relationship start intensely, followed by a steep drop in your partner's approval?

6. Have your friends and family commented that this relationship isn't healthy for you?

7. Does your relationship feel like an emotional roller coaster with patterns of high highs and low lows?

8. Is there a history of abuse in your family of origin, or were any family members ever diagnosed with a cluster B personality disorder (borderline, antisocial, histrionic, or narcissistic)?

9. Do you have a history of abusive relationships that cycle between phases of idealization, devaluation, and discarding?

10. Does your partner say that most issues in the relationship are your fault or blame you for having the "wrong" feelings?

11. Does your partner pretend to apologize but fail to take responsibility for their actions and blame you instead?

12. Does your partner habitually cheat or engage in other forms of dishonesty, or do they obsessively accuse you of cheating even though they are the ones with unaccounted time?

13. When you bring up unacceptable behavior to your partner, do they tell you that you're being too sensitive?

If your client answers in the affirmative to any of these questions, they may be experiencing gaslighting in their relationship. Consider asking your client to elaborate on their experiences to gain insight into their current relationship. Depending on the length of the relationship, your client may also have experienced other forms of abuse.

Are You Experiencing Gaslighting?

Gaslighting can appear in many sneaky and covert ways. To determine whether your partner's behaviors toward you are toxic and potentially qualify as gaslighting, put a check mark by any of the following statements that apply to you.

- ☐ This person has told me that I am crazy or that other people think I'm crazy.

- ☐ Trusted friends and loved ones are concerned about my relationship.

- ☐ This person has told me that friends and loved ones have said horrible things about me.

- ☐ I suspect this person is hiding my items and blaming me for losing them.

- ☐ This person is very focused on whether I am cheating, with no reason to suspect this.

- ☐ This person has told me that I am irresponsible with money and must turn over my finances to them.

- ☐ This person has told me we must go to couples therapy to figure out what is wrong with me.

- ☐ This person often tells me that what I have seen or heard didn't happen.

- ☐ When I set boundaries with this person, they blame me and get very angry.

- ☐ I have caught this person in lies that don't even make sense.

- ☐ I was treated exceptionally well at the beginning of the relationship, but now I am mistreated.

If you identified with one or more of these statements, you might be experiencing gaslighting. Your therapist can help you determine whether you have been subjected to this form of emotional abuse.

Copyright © 2024 Sarkis Media LLC, *A Clinician's Guide to Gaslighting*. All rights reserved.

Characteristics of Gaslighters

The following are characteristics of gaslighters—people who manipulate you into questioning your reality. To determine whether gaslighting may be occurring in one of the relationships in your life, put a check mark by any red flags you have noticed about this person:

❒ They are focused on their social status.

❒ They look good on paper (e.g., educated, accomplished), but the facts don't add up.

❒ They have substance abuse issues.

❒ They have control issues.

❒ They are quick to anger.

❒ They always talk about themselves.

❒ They refuse accountability for their behavior.

❒ They are generally dishonest and lie about trivial things.

❒ Their stories are constantly changing.

❒ They have cynical, negative views of others.

❒ They make promises but don't follow through.

❒ They blame you for being upset at their inappropriate behavior.

❒ They seem to "mirror" your likes and dislikes.

❒ They deny that you saw or heard them do something.

❒ They don't manage their finances well.

❒ They vilify their ex.

❒ They put their ex up on a pedestal.

❒ They believe that everything is always someone else's fault.

❒ They punish, shame, and guilt you.

❒ They showered you with attention and affection early on in the relationship but quickly became confrontational.

❒ They threaten suicide if you set boundaries or tell them you are leaving them.

❒ They lack any long-lasting friends.

❒ They boast about their "excellent" relationship with their children but rarely see them.

Even if you only checked a few of these items, this relationship might not be healthy for you, so it is essential to speak to your therapist about your experiences.

Copyright © 2024 Sarkis Media LLC, *A Clinician's Guide to Gaslighting*. All rights reserved.

Common Phrases of Gaslighters

If you are in a toxic relationship characterized by gaslighting, you may have heard the other person make the following comments. These statements usually fall under the acronym FOG—fear, obligation, and guilt—because they are meant to scare you, make you feel like you owe the other person, or make you feel like you have done something wrong. Put a check mark by any phrases that you have experienced in your relationship.

❏ Why can't you take a joke?

❏ You're so sensitive.

❏ Maybe you're the gaslighter.

❏ Everyone thinks you're crazy.

❏ No wonder your [*sister, brother, mother, father, etc.*] can't stand you.

❏ What you think you saw or heard never happened.

❏ Who are they going to believe, you or me?

❏ After everything I've done for you!

❏ How can you honestly say you're a good person?

❏ You misinterpret everything.

❏ You used to be so fun; now look at you.

❏ What makes you think you have a right to be picky?

❏ I've only ever tried to help you.

Copyright © 2024 Sarkis Media LLC, *A Clinician's Guide to Gaslighting*. All rights reserved.

Fear, Obligation, and Guilt (FOG)

When someone gaslights you, you may notice that they use three tactics to get you under their power: fear, obligation, and guilt. The quicker you identify these three factors, the less likely you are to be susceptible to them. Here are a few examples of each:

Fear	Obligation	Guilt
• "Everyone thinks you're crazy." • "No one will believe you." • "It would be a shame if other people learned about your past."	• "I've spent so much time trying to make you happy. The least you could do is do what I'm asking of you." • "I've spent a lot of money on our home. You owe me this." • "You owe me some time out with friends."	• "Why are you always so mean to me?" • "Don't you feel sorry for me? Even at all?" • "Why can't you just let me be happy?"

When a gaslighter tries to manipulate you with these tactics, how should you respond? By *not* responding. Nothing you say will make the other person gaslight you less. A gaslighter will use *anything* you say against you, so the best thing to do is to walk away. As difficult as it may be to resist, know these three tactics are just that—tactics. They are not the truth. Remember that it is a choice to not buy into what the gaslighter is telling you. Not giving them a response sends the message that you aren't buying what they are selling. It's a powerful message that is best said with silence.

Is It Gaslighting or Poor Communication?

You may feel like the term *gaslighting* has become so common in everyday speech that it's unclear what it is and how it differs from a relationship characterized by poor communication. Couples with communication difficulties may regularly struggle to express their wants and needs, or have challenges reflecting on their partner's words; however, this does not necessarily indicate that either party has ill intent. They may simply lack effective communication or coping skills. In contrast, a gaslighter's goal is not to build mutual trust, understanding, and connection but to undermine and control their partner. In a gaslighting relationship, when the victim brings up an issue, they are ridiculed by the other person or told that they are "crazy," "weird," or "ridiculous" to have such a concern. The gaslighter may even tell the victim that these concerns are just a sign of the victim's craziness, given that gaslighters act out when someone sets or enforces boundaries with them.

Above all, there is a concerted effort in gaslighting relationships to make the victim question their reality. The gaslighter may even claim that there's nothing wrong with their abusive behavior. They are especially likely to make this claim if the victim considers leaving or is already walking out the door. In this case, the gaslighter is driven by their constant need for attention and ego-stroking to try to hoover the client back into the relationship. One of the ways they do this is by trying to normalize their dysfunctional behavior, such as telling the client that this is "how relationships work." Rarely will a gaslighter admit to a campaign of confusion and control over their victim. Their refusal to accept responsibility can make it nearly impossible to have a productive couples therapy session.

Gaslighting or Poor Communication?

If you are having difficulties with your partner, you may wonder whether you are experiencing the regular "bumps" of a relationship or if there is more reason to be concerned. How do you know whether you are experiencing difficulties with communication or your partner is gaslighting you? Here are some ways to tell the difference:

Gaslighting	Poor Communication
• Your partner has an ulterior motive that involves wanting to control you or get away with something.	• You and your partner have difficulty expressing your needs and listening to each other.
• They lie to you or purposefully leave out information to gain an advantage over you.	• You aren't knowledgeable about practical communication skills such as active listening.
• They make promises they know they can't deliver as a way to maintain their narcissistic supply.	• The same point is brought up continuously with no progress in the discussion.
• They tell you that what you saw or heard never happened.	• A person's statements are misunderstood or misinterpreted.
• They use your fears and insecurities as ammunition against you.	• Clarification is not sought when a partner makes a confusing statement.
• Their actions don't match their words.	• Resentment toward your partner prevents productive discussion.
• They accuse you of things you didn't do.	• You continue a dialogue with your partner even though you need a short break.
• They yell or scream at you.	

Trust your gut instinct or intuition. If something feels wrong in your relationship, there is cause for concern.

 Copyright © 2024 Sarkis Media LLC, *A Clinician's Guide to Gaslighting*. All rights reserved.

DARVO

When someone experiences conflict in a healthy relationship, they can raise concerns with their partner and discuss the issue maturely and thoughtfully. But if your client is in a relationship characterized by gaslighting, they are likely to experience the following pattern of behavior if they confront their abuser:

- **Deny:** The victim is told that what they saw or heard never happened.
    - "I never said (or did) that."
    - "You're imagining things."
- **Attack:** The gaslighter goes on the offensive and attacks the victim.
    - "You've got issues."
    - "You're crazy."
- **Reverse Victim and Offender:** The gaslighter reverses the behavior, portraying themselves as the victim, while the actual victim is described as the offender.
    - "You're the one who is constantly accusing me of cheating."
    - "You always tell me that people think I'm crazy."
    - "I don't know why you attack me like this after everything I've done for you."
    - "I don't know how much more of this I can take from you."
    - "You constantly abuse me. Why?"
    - "I need to talk to someone about this toxic relationship."

Therefore, while you may be tempted to recommend that the client confront their gaslighter about their behavior, a safer way for the client to cope is to distance themselves as much as possible from the perpetrator of this abuse. You can find more information about going no-contact and low-contact in chapter 6.

DARVO

If you confront a gaslighter about their behavior, they usually respond in a pattern called DARVO, which stands for *deny*, *attack*, and *reverse victim and offender*.

- **Deny:** They tell you it never happened.

- **Attack:** They go after your behavior.

- **Reverse:** They blame you for the same offense.

- **Victim:** They make themselves the victim by guilting and shaming you.

- **Offender:** They have now made you out to be the villain.

Here is an example of how DARVO can play out:

> TANIA: I'm upset with how you spoke to me last night. It was unacceptable.
>
> HUGO: What are you talking about? We were fine last night. (*Deny*)
>
> TANIA: You called me a name and told me I was useless.
>
> HUGO: You always do this. You get abusive and claim I abused you. (*Attack*)
>
> TANIA: But I'm telling you exactly what happened. You called me a horrible name.
>
> HUGO: If I remember correctly, *you* called *me* some choice names last night. (*Reverse*)
>
> TANIA: No, I didn't! That's a lie!
>
> HUGO: If only you respected me and our relationship. I've tolerated so much. (*Victim*)
>
> TANIA: I do respect you and our relationship! Why are you doing this?
>
> HUGO: I don't know how much more of your abusive behavior I can take. (*Offender*)

Have you experienced DARVO in your relationship with a gaslighter? Describe your experience.

_____

_____

_____

_____

_____

_____

_____

Copyright © 2024 Sarkis Media LLC, *A Clinician's Guide to Gaslighting.* All rights reserved.

CHAPTER 2

Goals of Treatment

Perpetrators of emotional abuse want their victims to become dependent on them and believe they cannot function alone. Gaslighters accomplish this by drawing their victims into a web of deceit and isolation where they gradually distance the victim from trusted family members and friends. Some victims, under duress, even end up signing their financial accounts over to the abuser, who tells them they are too irresponsible. This abuse inevitably leads to money being withheld from the victim and the victim being forced to earn an "allowance" while the abuser spends the cash. For clients to heal, they must develop greater independence and differentiate themselves from the gaslighter.

In this chapter, you will learn the primary treatment goals when working with a victim of gaslighting, including how to help them take actionable steps that move them toward these goals. You will also explore the importance of providing your client with a detailed consent form and description of their rights. Finally, you will learn how to meet your client where they are and work at their own pace, including knowing when it is appropriate to use the word *abuse* to describe their experiences.

Treatment Goals

One of the main goals in treating survivors of emotional abuse is to increase their autonomy and independence. You want to enhance their ability to make decisions for themselves (and to feel responsibly adept at doing so) and help them know when they can solve an issue independently versus when they need more support. The more independent your client becomes, the more effectively they will make decisions. Independence begets autonomy.

Another goal of treatment is to help clients work through other traumas they have endured, as gaslighting can trigger memories of abuse. For many clients, their current relationship is just one of many traumas they have experienced. Some traumas may be related to past relationships, while others may be unrelated. Either way, these traumas likely contribute to a lack of predictability and an abundance of chaos—the same as in the gaslighting relationship. As a clinician, you must provide a safe space for your client to process past trauma, which you will learn more about in chapter 7.

Overall, your goals are to:

• Help your client heal from abuse

• Teach your client how to create and maintain boundaries

- Provide support when your client considers returning to their partner
- Discover the family of origin issues that may have made your client vulnerable to a toxic person
- Identify cognitive dissonance regarding the destructive nature of the relationship
- Help your client rebuild their life

When your client has been traumatized, developing rapport is also crucial. Your client may be new to the therapeutic process, as the gaslighter may have prevented them from seeking help in the past. Therefore, it is essential to emphasize the client's autonomy and independence throughout therapy by giving them full informed consent. Full informed consent includes letting your client know that they can discontinue treatment at any time without penalty. You need to meet the client where they are and move at their own pace, or they may shut down.

What Would You Like to Get Out of Therapy?

Everyone has different reasons for attending therapy. Usually, it has to do with having a better future for yourself, including changing patterns of behavior that no longer work for you. You may also see a therapist to talk through some difficult experiences that have happened to you. Although you may have heard from loved ones that therapy can help you, you might not know what to expect. Use the rest of this page to write about what you would like to get out of therapy. You can also add how you will know if therapy is working for you.

_____

_____

_____

_____

_____

_____

_____

_____

_____

_____

_____

_____

_____

_____

_____

_____

_____

_____

_____

_____

_____

How Would Your Life Be If
Things Were Going Well?

A helpful way to determine what you want to get out of therapy is to answer this question: How would your life be if things were going well? A good place to start is to consider: What would be the first thing you'd notice if you woke up tomorrow and everything was how you wanted it to be? Describe this in detail here, then continue writing about the rest of your day. Be as specific as possible. When you're done, share with your therapist as much of your response as you feel comfortable discussing.

_____

_____

_____

_____

_____

_____

_____

_____

_____

_____

_____

_____

_____

_____

_____

_____

_____

_____

_____

_____

_____

_____

_____

Copyright © 2024 Sarkis Media LLC, _A Clinician's Guide to Gaslighting_. All rights reserved.

Creating Goals for Your Client

If your client has been subjected to gaslighting, they may have difficulty creating goals for themselves. After all, the gaslighter has led them to believe they aren't worthy of their dreams, preferences, or thoughts. To help your client brainstorm goals for themselves, try using their answers from the previous worksheet, which focuses on the miracle question from solution-focused therapy: "How would your life be if things were going well?" and work backward from there.

Since it can be confusing to explain the difference between objectives and goals, look for other ways to describe it. For example, the following client worksheet uses the analogy of a staircase: A goal is the top of the stairs—where the client wishes to go—while objectives are the steps or measurable actions to help get them there. You may need to explain to your client that while it may feel like they are going up the staircase alone, you are a guide for them along the way. Having your client make their own goals and objectives (with your guidance) and reviewing their progress throughout therapy is vital to building your client's autonomy and independence.

Your Goals for Therapy

You can think of therapy like climbing a staircase: At the top of the stairs is the goal you want to achieve through your work in therapy. In order to reach the top, you will need to take multiple steps that support your goal, which we call objectives.

In the diagram that follows, write down your ultimate goal at the top of the stairs. For example, your goal might be to heal from a gaslighting relationship. Then, on the steps leading to the top of the staircase, write down the actions you can take to help you achieve that goal. Your objectives to help you heal from a gaslighting relationship might be to:

- Go no-contact with the person who has gaslit you

- Reconnect with supportive friends and family

- Learn more about gaslighting behaviors so you can avoid them in the future

- Identify and clarify your values in life

- Enforce healthier boundaries and learn to say no to others

- Acknowledge and validate your feelings

- Rediscover your autonomy and independence

- Attend psychotherapy consistently

Try to be kind to yourself while completing this exercise. As you think about what you would like to change in your life, you might feel discouraged, ashamed, or overwhelmed by your past or present experiences. Know that wherever you are now—and whatever you're feeling—is okay, and that starting therapy is itself an incredibly important step that you've already taken. Try not to critique yourself, and ask your therapist for assistance if needed. When you have finished this worksheet, share it with your therapist so they can better help you along your journey. They can also offer suggestions to refine your objectives to make it even more likely that you will achieve your goal.

Copyright © 2024 Sarkis Media LLC, *A Clinician's Guide to Gaslighting*. All rights reserved.

Goal:

Objectives:

What Is Therapy Like?

If you haven't been to therapy before, it can initially seem awkward and uncomfortable. You are meeting with a stranger to talk about experiences you may not have shared with your closest friends and family. You may also come from a family that discourages going to therapy, or your partner may have threatened to leave you or even hurt you if you talked about your relationship with a mental health professional. They may even have told you, "No one will believe you anyway" or "If you say something, I'll lose my job, and we'll be homeless. Is that what you want?"

However, the reality is that therapy is a safe space where you can share your innermost thoughts and feelings. Think of going to therapy as having coffee with someone who has no biases. A therapist is a neutral, trained professional. You have confidentiality in your sessions, meaning that what you say to your therapist is not shared with anyone else. These are the only exceptions that would require a therapist to break confidentiality:

- A judge subpoenas your therapist.

- You sign a release of information allowing your therapist to talk to the specific people noted on the release form (but no one else).

- You disclose to your therapist that you are considering harming yourself or others.

You can ask your therapist at your first session about the limitations of confidentiality. A good therapist encourages you to ask questions. If you feel uncomfortable or wonder why your therapist said something, bring this up to them. And remember that you can stop therapy at any time, for any reason, without adverse consequences from your therapist.

     Copyright © 2024 Sarkis Media LLC, *A Clinician's Guide to Gaslighting*. All rights reserved.

A Detailed Informed Consent Form

It is essential to provide your client with a detailed informed consent form to emphasize your client's autonomy and independence in session. A consent form for therapy should include the following:

- A description of the purpose of therapy

- Indicators that the client may no longer need therapy

- A notice of session fees and whether insurance is accepted

- An acknowledgment that participation in treatment is entirely voluntary

- An explanation of confidentiality and exceptions to it (such as a subpoena from a judge)

- Your theoretical orientation

- Your licenses and certifications

- The names and contact information for your licensing and credentialing boards

- Your office hours and locations

- Your policy on returning calls

- A statement that confidentiality can never be guaranteed with any form of electronic communication, including HIPAA-compliant video services

- Fees for no-showing or canceling within 24 hours of the session

- Costs for any letters requested, including for social security disability

- Online portal procedures and policies

- Signature and date lines for both you and your client

It is best to send your client a copy of the consent form before their appointment so they have time to read it. Then review it with them in session and invite them to ask any questions. When you are done, the client should be given a copy of the signed and dated consent form if it is not uploaded into a portal for them to download.

Your Rights in Therapy

You have the following rights in therapy:

- To end treatment at any time without repercussions

- To be spoken to with courtesy and respect

- To cancel or reschedule without penalty if it is done more than 24 hours in advance

- To ask questions about your therapist's training and education

- To ask questions about anything that occurs during your sessions

- To receive an informed consent document that states your rights and your therapist's office policies

- To get a therapist referral if you would like to try another therapist

Your therapist has rights as well:

- To be spoken to with courtesy and respect

- To challenge you without crossing boundaries

- To charge you the full amount of the session if you no-show or cancel within 24 hours

- To not schedule another appointment for you until you have paid your session fee

- To not schedule another session until your balance is paid in full

- To refer you to another therapist if they feel someone else would be a better fit for you or has more extensive training in a particular area

If at any time you have questions, feel free to ask your therapist. A good therapist will gladly answer your questions or let you know they don't have the answer but will do some research and get back to you.

Copyright © 2024 Sarkis Media LLC, *A Clinician's Guide to Gaslighting.* All rights reserved.

Boundary Crossings and Violations in Therapy

Part of knowing your rights in therapy is understanding the difference between a boundary crossing and a boundary violation. This handout provides you with information about both.

A **boundary crossing** can occur when you encounter your therapist outside of your appointments. This might happen for many reasons; here are some examples:

- You and your therapist are members of the same professional organization.

- Your children and your therapist's children are in the same class or after-school program.

- You and your therapist belong to the same gym.

- You and your therapist attend the same 12-step program.

Although boundary crossings aren't necessarily ethical violations, they should be avoided to the extent possible to prevent what is known as a "dual relationship." For example, if you and your therapist belong to the same gym, your therapist may ask you what times you usually work out so they can go at a different time. However, it's not always possible for your therapist to avoid seeing you outside of sessions, especially if you live in a smaller city or community. Either way, remember that your therapist won't say hello to you in public unless you do so first. It may feel like your therapist is ignoring you, but they are protecting your confidentiality. Your therapist will also address any potential boundary crossings in your sessions; for the time being, they may also not participate in the activity causing the boundary crossing.

Boundary violations occur when a therapist engages in unethical (and sometimes illegal) behaviors that harm or exploit you. A boundary violation has happened if your therapist:

- Tells you the name or other identifying information about another client

- Talks with your family, healthcare providers, or friends about your issues without a release of information

- Engages in any sexual activity with you

- Touches you without your consent

- Pressures you to buy their products

- Threatens you when you tell them you want to stop therapy

An ethical therapist will not cross these boundaries and abuse their power. If you ever receive treatment from a therapist who exhibits any of these behaviors, discontinue therapy and consider reporting them to their licensing board. Then contact another mental health professional to discuss any trauma you may have experienced due to the boundary violation.

Copyright © 2024 Sarkis Media LLC, *A Clinician's Guide to Gaslighting.* All rights reserved.

Your Rights as a Person

When you've been in a relationship with a toxic person, been raised by one, or worked for one, that person most likely consistently violated your boundaries. When you are around someone who doesn't have your best interests in mind, it can be easy to forget your rights. As a human, you have the following rights:

- The right to say no

- The right to change your mind at any time

- The right to do less than what is humanly possible

- The right to feel safe

- The right to state your needs and wants

- The right to distance yourself from toxic people

- The right to end a conversation at any time

- The right to have joy in your life

- The right to have your needs met without guilt or shame

- The right to know yourself as a person worthy of love and respect

Which of these rights stand out to you? Perhaps there is one that feels especially important to you now, or one that you hadn't realized was a right because you were told you must do something to "earn" it. You might also think of other rights to add to the list. Write your reflections here:

_____

_____

_____

_____

_____

_____

_____

Look back at this list if you ever feel unsure about what you have the right to ask for in a relationship, at work, or with family. You have a right to be treated with kindness and respect.

Copyright © 2024 Sarkis Media LLC, *A Clinician's Guide to Gaslighting*. All rights reserved.

The Importance of Working at Your Client's Pace

Although you may want to use the word *abuse* to describe a client's experiences, it may be too early for some clients to feel comfortable acknowledging that they were, in fact, in an abusive relationship. Follow your client's lead. It is best to let the client come to their own realization that they experienced abuse, and there is no set timeline for doing so. Although gentle confrontation can be healthy in moving your client forward, you want to steer clear of following your agenda and pushing your client before they are ready. Just listening to your client often provides them with the support they need. Remember that you may be the first person they have shared this information with.

With other terminology as well, it is best to ask your client what they would prefer if you are unsure whether a word is appropriate. For example, some clients may choose the term *toxic* instead of *abusive*, or *survivor* instead of *victim*. In addition, your client may use a derogatory term (such as "jerk" or "asshole") when referring to the gaslighter in session rather than using the person's real name. It is normal for clients to use such nicknames, and this can even help them regain their power. It is also a way for clients to express their anger toward the gaslighter. It is up to you if you want to use that term or if you would rather refer to the gaslighter in terms of their connection to your client, such as "your mother" or "your partner."

Although you may feel like your client isn't making progress at times, they may only be in the disclosing stage of their therapeutic journey—which is to say that you may be there to plant the seeds of progress. Another clinician may help your former client sow the seeds of that work at a later date. It doesn't mean you did anything wrong. Remember that gaslighting victims are caught in a cycle of abuse, so it is common for them to make several unsuccessful attempts to leave the abusive relationship before they leave for good, if they are indeed ever able to do so (see chapter 6 for more information on the trauma bond). Ultimately, you are there to provide support and guidance, not "fix" your client's issues. Attempting to fix a client's issues robs them of learning the essential steps toward independence and autonomy.

Your Experiences with Clients
and the Word *Abuse*

There is an art to knowing when clients are ready to hear the word *abuse* used to describe their relationship with a gaslighter. It is essential to meet your client where they are in treatment and to work at their pace while occasionally gently challenging them. The following prompts will help you reflect on your use of the word *abuse* when working with clients.

Have you ever used the word *abuse* with a client before they were ready? Describe this experience.

_____

_____

_____

_____

_____

How did you resolve this interaction with your client?

_____

_____

_____

_____

_____

What are some ways in which you have followed (or would like to follow) your clients' lead when using the word *abuse*?

_____

_____

_____

_____

_____

Copyright © 2024 Sarkis Media LLC, *A Clinician's Guide to Gaslighting*. All rights reserved.

CHAPTER 3

Who Perpetrates Gaslighting?

Gaslighters come from all genders, cultures, ages, socioeconomic levels, and other demographics. Most commonly, gaslighters qualify for a cluster B personality disorder or, at the very least, exhibit qualities inherent to these disorders, such as lack of empathy. Clients themselves can also be perpetrators of gaslighting, especially if they have "fleas" from their family of origin, meaning that they carry remnants of their parents' abusive behaviors into their relationships. People in various types of relationships and contexts can perpetrate gaslighting too. While gaslighting is most commonly associated with toxic or abusive intimate relationships, it can also occur in families, friendships, workplaces, and society at large. Anyone can engage in gaslighting behaviors, and no one is immune to the damage this type of abuse can cause.

In this chapter, you'll learn about the connection between cluster B personality disorders, gaslighting, and covert and overt narcissism. You'll discover how difficult it is to detect covert narcissism at the beginning of a relationship and learn what happens when your client self-identifies as a gaslighter. Unlike clients with narcissistic personality disorder, self-identifying gaslighters know that some of their behaviors are not conducive to healthy relationships. Many of these clients have "fleas" that they unknowingly carry into their current relationships. Finally, you'll explore how you might be carrying gaslighting behaviors as well, which is why it is crucial to engage in self-examination if you are to be the best clinician for your clients.

Cluster B Personality Disorders and Gaslighting

The cluster B personality disorders—borderline, histrionic, antisocial, and narcissistic—are characterized by unstable emotions, impulsive behaviors, intense interpersonal relationships, and self-centeredness (APA, 2022). The connection between these disorders and gaslighting lies in the manipulative and controlling behaviors that characterize both. For example, people with borderline personality disorder struggle with intense emotions, a strong fear of abandonment, an unstable sense of self, and often a history of sexual abuse. To maintain control and attempt to decrease their level of emotional distress due to potential abandonment, they may resort to gaslighting others by denying their actions, distorting facts, pitting people against each other, threatening suicide, or shifting blame onto others.

Similarly, people with narcissistic personality disorder exhibit an exaggerated sense of self-importance and lack empathy, which can contribute to gaslighting as they try to distort reality to maintain a sense of superiority and control over others. By gaslighting, they invalidate the experiences and emotions of their victims, making them question their perceptions and feelings. This is a tactic often used by people with antisocial personality disorder as well, who use gaslighting to gain power and erode their victims' sense of self and autonomy. Finally, people with histrionic personality disorder may use gaslighting to seek attention, create drama, or stir up confrontation. Although their intentions are not typically as hostile as those with antisocial or narcissistic traits, individuals with histrionic personality disorder will still use manipulative tactics as a way to remain the center of attention.

Addressing gaslighting within cluster B personality disorders requires clients to be willing to explore and challenge their maladaptive behaviors, accept responsibility for past behaviors, develop empathy and emotional regulation skills, and create healthy communication and relationship patterns. However, this can prove difficult given that people with personality disorders have *ego-syntonic* personalities, meaning they do not believe they have a problem. This is in contrast to people with *ego-dystonic* personalities, who feel uncomfortable or guilty when they do something inconsistent with their beliefs and values, leading them to make amends or seek the help of a mental health professional. The ego-syntonic nature of personality disorders is one of the reasons they are challenging to treat in therapy.

Clients with personality disorders are also not very likely to attend therapy unless it is court-ordered or their partner forces them into couples counseling. Or they might seek out therapy, but as a way to bring their partner to session and blame them for any issues in the relationship. Any attempts you make to ask a person with a cluster B personality disorder how they have contributed to the relationship will likely be met with rage, stonewalling, or deflection. They may deflect with statements of victimhood, such as "The only thing I am guilty of is trying so hard to make this work" and "I'm only responsible for loving her too much to leave." Remember that these comments are not genuine and are projections of how they treat their partner.

It is important to note that not all individuals with cluster B personality disorders engage in gaslighting, and not all gaslighters have a diagnosable personality disorder. However, the characteristics and behaviors associated with these disorders can increase the likelihood that a client will engage in gaslighting behaviors. By that same token, if a client's gaslighting behavior is infrequent and limited in scope, it may indicate that they do not meet diagnostic criteria for a cluster B personality disorder. Some abusers will only engage in gaslighting if something triggers their anxious or avoidant attachment style (see chapter 5). However, a victim never "causes" abusive behavior from the gaslighter. Gaslighters are still 100 percent responsible for their behavior, regardless of how they came to that behavior.

Covert and Overt Narcissism

While overt and covert narcissism aren't discussed in the latest edition of the *Diagnostic and Statistical Manual of Mental Disorders* (DSM-5; APA, 2022), it is generally accepted that these are the two main types of narcissism. Overt narcissists are characterized by their grandiose, attention-seeking, and entitled personalities. These individuals demand special treatment and don't care if others witness their fits of rage. This behavior reflects the classic form of narcissism that people usually have in mind when they think of narcissistic personality disorder. These individuals often may:

- Dress in a "flashy" way

- Express anger publicly

- Be loud in social gatherings

- Try to "one up" others in conversation

- Be focused on acquiring status symbols

- Have poor money management skills

- Appear extraverted

- Become aggressive and violent when angry

- Feel they should be entitled to different rules of behavior

- Outwardly mock others

- Behave rudely to people they deem as "less worthy," such as waitstaff

In contrast, covert narcissists can be more challenging to spot, especially during the idealization phase, since they don't portray themselves with the same aggrandizing self-importance. Instead, they tend to be self-pitying and play the martyr in relationships. Because it can be challenging to identify covert narcissism, many mental health professionals unknowingly enter into therapeutic relationships with these clients, only to discover their true persona after a boundary is enforced and narcissistic behaviors emerge. These individuals generally:

- Are self-deprecating (make fun of themselves but in a very negative way)

- Are reserved and quiet

- Express anger in a closed (non-public) setting

- Blame others for their own mistakes

- Engage in "trauma dumping" early in the relationship, whereby they overshare their traumatic or difficult experiences with the other person

- Talk about their piety (how "good" or religious they are)

- Exhibit passive-aggressive behavior when angry

- Incessantly complain about others

- Seem quiet and unassuming until they don't get what they want

- Show narcissistic rage through stonewalling and "punishment"

- Are more likely to deflect during therapy than storm out

- Appear introverted

- Are more likely to be female than overt narcissists (Green et al., 2020)

Although covert and overt narcissists present differently, they are two sides of the same coin in that they are both characterized by an injured ego and a belief that they are better than others. That is why gaslighting is often exhibited by both types of narcissists. They use gaslighting to punish others and mask their deep-seated insecurities. Gaslighting is also a way for them to distract their victims and avoid taking responsibility for their abusive behaviors.

As a clinician, it is crucial to be mindful of how these two different presentations can manifest in the therapy hour. For example, if an overt narcissist shows up late for their appointment, they may rage when you can't give them a full hour of your time. On the other hand, a covert narcissist may not say anything at the time but then express their displeasure by no-showing at their next appointment or refusing to answer your calls. Be clear with your boundaries at the outset of therapy and know that it is your right as a clinician to discharge a client who will not or cannot respect your boundaries and the limits of the therapeutic relationship.

In many cases, you may not see the gaslighter at all in therapy. While you cannot diagnose someone you are not working with, it can be very empowering for your client if you educate them about the signs of overt and covert narcissism, allowing them to notice for themselves whether their gaslighter's behavior aligns with these characteristics.

Is Your Gaslighter a Covert or Overt Narcissist?

Gaslighting and narcissism often go hand in hand. However, while some gaslighters have overt (obvious or outward) narcissistic traits, others are more difficult to identify because they have covert (hidden or inward) narcissistic traits. Put a check mark by any of the following characteristics that fit the gaslighter in your life.

☐   1.   They play the victim and blame others for their behavior.

☐   2.   They are obsessed with appearances.

☐   3.   They give you the silent treatment or stonewall you when angry.

☐   4.   They mock others in public.

☐   5.   They react to anger with passive-aggressive behavior.

☐   6.   They make a scene when their demands aren't met.

☐   7.   They "trauma dump," telling you deeply personal information early in the relationship.

☐   8.   They make public displays of their "good deeds."

☐   9.   They act out only when you set a boundary.

☐   10.   They demand loyalty but never give it in return.

☐   11.   They blame most of their past relationship difficulties solely on their ex-partners.

☐   12.   They tell you that what you saw and heard isn't what happened.

☐   13.   They make a point of telling you about their good values and morals.

☐   14.   They undermine your parenting in front of you.

☐   15.   They hide your cherished belongings and say you may have memory issues.

☐   16.   They share your vulnerabilities with others while you are present.

☐   17.   They often complain to you about others' "faults."

☐   18.   They tell you they don't have enough money but buy themselves expensive gifts.

☐   19.   They cheat on you but are very good at hiding it.

☐   20.   They blatantly cheat on you, telling you to "deal with it or leave."

You might be dealing with a covert narcissist if you checked off more odd-numbered items, while you might be dealing with an overt narcissist if you checked off more even-numbered items. Discuss your findings from this quiz with your therapist to learn more about narcissism and how you can respond to the gaslighter in your life.

Copyright © 2024 Sarkis Media LLC, *A Clinician's Guide to Gaslighting.* All rights reserved.

The Profile of a Self-Aware Gaslighter

You may occasionally have potential clients who contact you because they believe *they* might be a gaslighter. They may tell you that they read a book on the topic, saw a video on social media, or had a trusted friend tell them they were engaging in gaslighting. Many will detail how their behaviors have led to relationship and workplace difficulties. Although it is possible that some of these clients may exhibit signs of covert or overt narcissism, if they take responsibility for their behaviors, it likely indicates that they are experiencing "fleas" instead. In this case, the ego-syntonic behavior seen in narcissistic personality disorder is absent, which means these clients have a good chance of improving.

The following are some qualities of the self-aware gaslighter:

- They feel protective toward their abusive family of origin.
- They dissociate during a session when discussing past trauma.
- They have few or brief romantic relationships.
- They feel lonely and lack friendships.
- They are very open about their experiences from the beginning of therapy.
- They overly blame themselves.
- They have strained relationships with their siblings.
- They feel crushing guilt and shame.
- They have suicidal ideation or plans.

If you are working with a client who presents as a self-aware gaslighter, it is paramount that you create a safe and nonjudgmental therapy environment. It takes tremendous courage for a gaslighter to recognize and acknowledge that the behaviors they learned in childhood are negatively impacting their relationships today. Acknowledge their bravery in reaching out for help. As you work together, an essential part of treatment will involve examining how they may have unknowingly picked up these manipulative behaviors, or fleas, from their parents or caregivers while growing up. You'll learn more about how to work through family of origin issues in chapter 5.

Reactive or Defensive Abuse

When working with a victim of emotional abuse, there may be times when your client lashes out against their abuser. This behavior is known as *reactive abuse* or *defensive abuse*, and it occurs when someone defends themselves or reacts with violence because they have been backed into a corner, blocked from leaving, or continually verbally or physically attacked. They may yell, hurl insults, and even physically retaliate against the abuser. Reactive abuse is a self-defense mechanism that gaslighting victims resort to when caught in a cycle of abuse. Sometimes a victim knows the pattern of abuse is about to occur, and their fear and trepidation can be just as tormenting as the abuse. The victim may then engage in reactive abuse to trigger the abuse cycle and finish it more quickly.

The following are signs of reactive or defensive abuse:

- The client's actions were preceded by abuse from a partner or family member.

- The client was blamed by their partner after the abuse.

- The gaslighter brings up the reactive abuse after the incident as a guilt and shame tactic.

- The gaslighter labels your client as abusive or claims that your client is the gaslighter (see the description of DARVO in chapter 1).

- The client feels excessive shame and guilt after they engage in defensive abuse.

It is essential to explain to clients that there is a clear difference between the type of emotional abuse perpetrated by a gaslighter versus the reactive abuse the client may engage in once they've been pushed to their breaking point. If a client is convinced they are abusive, ask them about their prior history of violence. One question to determine the presence of reactive or defensive abuse is "Have you ever instigated abuse?" Often, you'll find that clients who have engaged in reactive or defensive abuse have never initiated the abusive behavior.

Reactive or Defensive Abuse

When you are in a toxic relationship, it is common for the gaslighter to tell you that *you* are the abusive one. Gaslighters may even portray themselves as victims of "your abusive behavior." If there are times that you lash out or fight back against the gaslighter in response to their abuse, this is known as *reactive abuse*. For example, the gaslighter may have backed you into a corner or blocked your exit, so you tried to push them away. Or they may have yelled at you while your faces were so close that they were almost touching, so you reacted by spitting on them to get them to back off. Or the gaslighter may have pressured you into slapping or hitting them and then said they couldn't believe how abusive you were.

When you respond to abuse by defending yourself, you are not an abuser. You are also not the abuser if you feel you "set off" the gaslighter to get the abuse over and done with. When you know that a blowup is about to happen, it is perfectly understandable that you would want to purposely trigger a confrontation instead of waiting in misery for the inevitable. Know that reactive abuse is not your fault. You were doing the best you could in an untenable situation.

You can use the space here to describe times that you may have engaged in reactive abuse. What led to these reactions?

_____

_____

_____

_____

_____

_____

_____

_____

_____

_____

_____

_____

_____

_____

_____

Copyright © 2024 Sarkis Media LLC, *A Clinician's Guide to Gaslighting*. All rights reserved.

Checking Your Countertransference Toward Gaslighters

When you are working with challenging clients who seem to provoke you or intentionally keep you feeling off-kilter, it can change how you treat them and others in your life (including other clients in your practice). The following are all signs that you may be experiencing countertransference toward a client who is a perpetrator of gaslighting:

- Making sarcastic or snide comments to your client
- Sabotaging your client by advising with unhelpful information
- Siding with your client's partner during a session
- Treating your significant other or spouse with contempt
- Having a short fuse with others in your life
- Having past trauma influence your sessions

If you are experiencing countertransference, seek the counsel of another mental health professional. It is normal to feel anger, resentment, and confusion toward highly manipulative clients. Consider referring them to another therapist, preferably someone specializing in cluster B personality disorders. If you are doing couples therapy, consider continuing therapy only with the non-gaslighting member of the couple. When transitioning from couples to individual therapy, be cautious about how you phrase this switch. The gaslighter will most likely use their termination from therapy as an excuse to emphasize that their partner is the "crazy one" who needs all the help. The gaslighter may also view your treatment of their partner as a threat, as you are helping the remaining client understand the pathology of the relationship. You may be able to mitigate this by explaining that sometimes it is more beneficial for each partner to work with their own therapist than to continue couples sessions that have not been productive.

Self-Reflection on Countertransference

Even the most seasoned therapists are not immune to countertransference, especially when working with challenging clients who have a history of gaslighting and other emotionally abusive behavior. Since these reactions can interfere with the therapeutic alliance, it is important to reflect on how you have overcome countertransference in the past and how you might address it in the future.

Describe a time when you experienced countertransference toward a challenging client, including the specific emotions, thoughts, and urges you had at the time. What about this client did you find triggering?

_____

_____

_____

Did this client remind you of someone in your past or something you experienced? If so, describe this person or experience. What is the resemblance or connection to the client?

_____

_____

_____

What challenges did you experience with this client, and how did you resolve the situation?

_____

_____

_____

How might the past experience you've described help you identify and address possible countertransference in the future?

_____

_____

_____

 Copyright © 2024 Sarkis Media LLC, *A Clinician's Guide to Gaslighting*. All rights reserved.

Checking Your Gaslighting Behaviors

While we all would prefer to believe that we never exhibit manipulative behaviors, chances are that it has happened at least a few times, whether in our personal or professional lives. Some clinicians may even unknowingly engage in gaslighting behaviors in the clinical setting when they try to cover up an error, or if they engage in unethical and illegal behavior and tell their clients that this is an acceptable part of the therapeutic process. Milder versions of gaslighting in a professional setting can look like the following:

- "No, I didn't double-book. You misheard the appointment time."
- "I must not have gotten your voicemail."
- "I never said that to you."
- "That chart note is accurate. That is what happened."

The origins of gaslighting behaviors in clinicians can vary. They can arise from personal trauma, professional burnout, inadequate supervision or training, addiction, or unresolved countertransference. In addition, clinicians who have experienced gaslighting or emotional abuse in their personal lives may unintentionally replicate those patterns in their interactions with clients. Here are some examples of gaslighting behaviors that clinicians may exhibit in session and potential reasons for these behaviors:

- **Minimizing and denial:** Clinicians may downplay or dismiss a client's experiences or emotions, making them doubt their reality. This behavior can occur when a clinician is uncomfortable with intense emotions, is afraid of addressing complex topics, or has personal biases that invalidate the client's perspective.

- **Blaming and shifting responsibility:** Clinicians may attribute a client's challenges only to their weaknesses or shortcomings, neglecting to consider external or systemic factors at play, such as an abusive family of origin. This behavior can occur when a clinician feels the need to exert control over the client and the session, or if they lack awareness of common environmental or societal factors that can affect clients.

- **Distorting facts and manipulation:** Clinicians may intentionally manipulate and distort information to maintain power or authority over the therapeutic relationship. By its nature, the therapeutic relationship already has an imbalance of power. A clinician who is willing to manipulate and distort information can be driven by their need for validation, the "high" they experience from gaining control, or a lack of ethical knowledge or understanding.

- **Undermining autonomy and independence:** Clinicians may subtly or overtly discourage their clients from seeking a second opinion, gaining alternate perspectives, making decisions, or asserting autonomy. This behavior can happen when a clinician exhibits a need for control, fears losing a client's dependence, is addicted to financial gain, or harbors professional insecurities.

- **Engaging in other boundary violations:** Clinicians may violate professional boundaries by breaking confidentiality, engaging in a dual relationship, using their position to manipulate or exploit the client, falsifying chart notes, or accepting gifts and favors in return for a favorable result in an evaluation. Boundary violations such as these may stem from a therapist's need for power and control, unresolved personal issues, or professional incompetence.

- **Clinician addiction issues:** If a clinician is experiencing issues with addictions, they may appear impaired or uncoordinated, talk with slurred speech, exhibit a change in their appearance, or smell like alcohol in session. If a client comments on this, the clinician may deny any issues with impairment, telling the client that they are mistaken or that they must be the ones that are impaired. Clinicians may engage in this behavior if they are entrenched in addiction, have unresolved psychological issues, and fear losing their job.

If a clinician has been engaging in gaslighting behaviors in the professional setting, it is essential that they seek the guidance of another mental health professional. They may also want to consult an attorney regarding any ethical and legal violations that have been reported to their respective licensing or credentialing board. Ultimately, clinicians must commit to professional growth, ethical practice, and clear boundaries. Complete knowledge of the laws, rules, and ethics of a clinician's license and certification is mandatory. "I didn't know" is not an adequate defense when accused of ethical wrongdoing. To provide a safe and empowering therapeutic environment for clients, clinicians must engage in continuous education on trauma-informed care, cultural competence, the laws and ethics of psychotherapy, and inherent power dynamics in the clinician-client relationship.

Have You Been Gaslighting Someone?

As a therapist, you may have engaged in destructive gaslighting behaviors toward family, friends, and clients without realizing it. Gaslighting behaviors can include "diagnosing" your partner with a mental health disorder when they are legitimately addressing a concern or telling your coworker that you heard other clinicians at the office saying she is terrible at her job. Behaviors like these make the other person question their reality.

Put a check mark by any of the following gaslighting behaviors you have engaged in:

- ❐ Spread lies about someone to impact their career or reputation

- ❐ Lied to a client about the time or date of a scheduled appointment

- ❐ Lied when you were a witness in court

- ❐ Were dishonest on a chart note

- ❐ Told a family member or partner that they were crazy or "diagnosed" them

- ❐ Used your clout as a clinician to manipulate someone

- ❐ Falsified billing documents to insurance companies

- ❐ Lied to a family member or partner about your whereabouts

- ❐ Hidden items from someone and blamed them for being irresponsible

- ❐ Told someone that what they saw or heard never happened

- ❐ Stole or used someone's possessions (food, office supplies, etc.) without permission, then denied it

- ❐ Told a coworker that they had to perform work tasks for you or you would report them to a supervisor

If you found yourself checking off many of these problematic behaviors, it is crucial that you engage in ongoing self-reflection, supervision, and continuing education. You will also benefit from exploring your biases and triggers in therapy. The earlier you get help for gaslighting behaviors, the better your outcome will be for helping your clients and leading a healthier life.

Copyright © 2024 Sarkis Media LLC, *A Clinician's Guide to Gaslighting.* All rights reserved.

CHAPTER 4

Interactions with Gaslighters

The deceit, abuse, and manipulation associated with gaslighting can make anyone question their sanity and lose their self-esteem. To isolate and control their victims, gaslighters engage in a specific pattern of behavior when interacting with their targets. In this chapter, you will discover the three stages of a gaslighting relationship—idealization, devaluation, and discarding—and explore the manipulation tactics that gaslighters use to keep their victims in an abusive relationship, including triangulation, splitting, weaponized guilt, and invisible armies.

The Cycle of a Gaslighter

In healthy, mutually respectful relationships, there is steadiness and consistency. While issues may arise, there are usually no big surprises, and both people are invested in working together to solve any problems. However, in toxic relationships characterized by gaslighting, three distinct phases describe the cycle of abuse—*idealization*, *devaluation*, and *discarding*—sometimes followed by a fourth phase called *hoovering*. This phased approach to manipulation occurs whether the relationship is romantic, platonic, familial, or professional.

Idealization

The idealization phase usually occurs at the beginning of a relationship or after a reconciliation. Love bombing is a key feature of this phase, in which the victim is placed on a pedestal and treated as if they can do no wrong. The following are some telltale signs of love bombing:

- Making grand gestures, such as public displays of affection and commitment
- Pushing for commitment, such as cohabitation, very early in the relationship
- Using superlatives to describe the client, such as *best* or *perfect*
- Mirroring many of the same attributes as the client, even down to specific interests
- Saying they find the client's weaknesses endearing or cute
- Bringing gifts to each date
- Asking repeatedly if the client is "100 percent committed" to being in a relationship

These love-bombing behaviors are a means to an end: to get your client hooked as quickly as possible. The gaslighter may tell your client, "You're the most amazing person I have ever met," "I've never met anyone like you," and "You're perfect." Hearing this praise can be intoxicating to the victim, particularly if they have experienced trauma and come from an abusive family of origin where recognition was rarely given. The idealization phase usually lasts until the victim enforces a boundary, officially commits to the relationship, or exhibits behavior that the gaslighter finds "disloyal."

Devaluation

Once the idealization phase ends, the devaluation phase begins as the gaslighter starts withdrawing affection and questioning the victim's reality. The victim goes from a person who seemingly can do no wrong in their partner's eyes to someone who apparently can do no right. They are pushed off their pedestal, degraded, and made to feel "less than." The emotional and verbal abuse accompanying this phase can segue into physical abuse, including pushing, shoving, hitting, pinching, blocking an exit, or excessive tickling.

Discarding

In the discarding phase, the gaslighter has already found other sources of narcissistic supply and may be engaged in multiple affairs. If the victim states that they find this behavior intolerable, the gaslighter may abruptly leave the victim or tell them, "You can leave if you don't like it. No one is forcing you to be here." However, if the victim leaves first, the gaslighter may attempt to hoover them back into the relationship. If the gaslighter is successful, the cycle starts all over again with the idealization phase.

Hoovering

Gaslighters seem to know precisely when their victims are most vulnerable, even years after their last contact. Hoovering (named after the vacuum) is the process by which the gaslighter sucks a victim back into contact with them. Many victims will say they finally felt like themselves, only for their gaslighter to reappear. When gaslighters hoover, they will seek any possible method of communication with your client. They may send a short text, post something on social media that references the relationship, or mail a "gift" or personal item to your client's home. If your client responds, the gaslighter's contact will ramp up quickly.

When this occurs, consider asking your client if they feel the gaslighter's behavior has truly changed. The gaslighter's sole purpose in hoovering is to fill their ego when they are low on narcissistic supply. If your client lets them back in, the gaslighter will be just as dysfunctional as before, and your client's relationship with them will become even more abusive. Your client must remain no-contact or low-contact even as the hoovering attempts get more frantic. It is also essential to discuss the trauma bond with your client, as this is a large part of what makes it so hard to stay away from a gaslighter (see chapter 6).

At any given moment in time, your client may be in a distinct stage of a gaslighting relationship or between stages. For example, if the relationship is still new, the victim may continue receiving positive reinforcement from their partner but also begin to receive criticism regarding their appearance or behaviors. It's essential to identify these stages and help your client determine where their relationship is in this cycle.

Which Relationship Phase Are You In?

Toxic relationships, including those with gaslighting, go through three phases: idealization, devaluation, and discarding. None of these stages is healthy; they only trap you into a cycle of abuse and manipulation. To determine which relationship phase you are in, read the following items and put a check mark by any that apply to your relationship.

- ☐   1.   This relationship is the best it's ever been, or it feels too good to be true.
- ☐   2.   I am being treated very, very well.
- ☐   3.   I am being showered with gifts.
- ☐   4.   I am being pressured into a commitment.
- ☐   5.   My partner has made criticisms about my appearance.
- ☐   6.   I am being compared to my siblings, my partner's ex, or my friends.
- ☐   7.   My items have gone missing, and I am told I am irresponsible.
- ☐   8.   I'm told that friends and family are saying bad things about me.
- ☐   9.   I am being accused of things I have never done.
- ☐ 10.   I have evidence that my partner is being unfaithful.
- ☐ 11.   I am being physically abused.
- ☐ 12.   I have been told I can leave the relationship if I don't like it.

To obtain a total score, tally the number of items you marked in each section:

Items 1 through 4: _____   Items 5 through 8: _____   Items 9 through 12: _____

If your total for items 1 through 4 was greater, you might be in the **idealization** phase of the relationship. This phase doesn't last, especially when you voice your needs or enforce a boundary.

If your total for items 5 through 8 was greater, you might be in the **devaluation** phase of the relationship. In this phase, criticism and gaslighting will continue to increase.

If your total for items 9 through 12 was greater, you might be in the **discard** phase of the relationship. You are at a critical point in the relationship where the chances of your partner's behavior becoming aggressive, violent, and even deadly have increased. Please consider going no-contact or low-contact with this person.

If you are experiencing any of these phases, your therapist can help you determine what you may need in order to extract yourself from this harmful relationship.

     Copyright © 2024 Sarkis Media LLC, *A Clinician's Guide to Gaslighting*. All rights reserved.

Signs of Hoovering

More often than not, when you cut off contact with a gaslighter, they will try to "hoover" or suck you back into a relationship. This behavior doesn't happen because the gaslighter loves or cares about you. It reflects the gaslighter's constant need for attention, validation, and admiration (known as "narcissistic supply"). If the gaslighter is not getting enough attention from other sources, it's easier for them to reach back out to you (their old supply) rather than find someone new. If you haven't blocked the gaslighter's phone number, email, and social media accounts, it is in your best interest to do so now.

Even still, the gaslighter may find an alternate way of contacting you, like getting another number or mailing something to your house. The message you receive may be anything from a simple "hey" to what appears to be an apology—even months or years after their bad behavior. However, the apology is often not genuine and reflects an attempt to lure you back into the cycle of emotional abuse. If you restart a relationship with them, you will likely find it just as dysfunctional as before (if not more so). The best way to stop hoovering is to ignore the gaslighter and avoid making contact with them. Rarely does responding end up in your favor. Going low-contact is an option if you cannot go no-contact, such as if you have children with the gaslighter.

The following are signs of hoovering:

- Sending a text message with just "hi" or "hey"

- Contacting you about an article or other item you might be "interested in"

- Contacting you for help with something "important"

- Posting memes on social media that are directed toward you

- Posting photos of their new narcissistic supply on social media

- Telling you that a pet you shared "misses you" and "wants to see you"

- Walking by your workplace or where you usually hang out with friends

- Sending another person ("flying monkey") with a message from them

Beware that hoovering behaviors may increase as the gaslighter realizes they have lost their source of narcissistic supply. Their behavior can cross into stalking, other forms of harassment, and violent behavior. You can report stalking to law enforcement, and depending on the severity of the stalking, you may qualify for a restraining order or an injunction. This legal document, signed by a judge, orders the person to stay away from your home and workplace. They are also not allowed to contact you in any way.

Copyright © 2024 Sarkis Media LLC, *A Clinician's Guide to Gaslighting.* All rights reserved.

Manipulation Tactics

Cognitive Empathy

Empathy is about being able to put yourself in another person's situation. There are two types of empathy: affective and cognitive. Affective empathy reflects the ability to share another person's emotional state, while cognitive empathy is the ability to understand another person's perspective. Although gaslighters may practice cognitive empathy, they lack affective empathy. In other words, they know what they are supposed to say to sound empathic, but there isn't any shared feeling behind the words. When gaslighters ask someone how they are feeling, they generally don't care to hear the answer. They are asking because they have been taught that people are supposed to be able to share in another person's experience. Their partner may also have threatened to leave if the gaslighter continues with their self-centered behavior.

Your clients may sometimes tell you that their partner has made a "breakthrough" because they asked about the client's feelings or inquired about their day. However, these breakthroughs are more likely to reflect love bombing or hoovering. They are ways the gaslighter is attempting to demonstrate that they have "changed" so their partner doesn't leave and they can maintain their source of narcissistic supply. To determine whether the gaslighter has truly changed, ask your client if their partner's facial expressions are congruent with their words. For example, when your client talks about a difficult part of their day, does their partner react with nonverbal gestures of concern (e.g., a furrowed brow, wrinkled nose)? Does their partner share in the client's pain? More likely than not, your client will notice that their facial expressions don't match. You may need to gently challenge clients in these instances to help them understand the true motivation behind the gaslighter's behavior.

Identifying Cognitive Empathy

There are two types of empathy: the ability to share in another person's feelings (*affective empathy*) and the ability to understand what they might be thinking (*cognitive empathy*). Some people don't feel others' emotions even though they are able to recognize or guess what others are feeling—these individuals may have cognitive empathy but not affective empathy. For example, you may know someone who claims to understand what you are feeling, but their nonverbals (their facial expression, body language, tone of voice, eye contact, etc.) do not match what they say.

Describe a time when someone sounded caring, but there wasn't any genuine feeling behind their words. What let you know the other person didn't truly empathize with your emotions?

_____

_____

_____

Does this person often have difficulty expressing intense emotions or accuse you of being "too sensitive"? Do they respond to your emotions with logical statements instead of actively listening to you?

_____

_____

_____

Does it feel like this person cannot or will not see things from your point of view? What are some examples of times when this has happened?

_____

_____

_____

Has this person used logic to twist your perception of events and ignored your emotions? If so, describe what that experience was like.

_____

_____

_____

Copyright © 2024 Sarkis Media LLC, *A Clinician's Guide to Gaslighting.* All rights reserved.

Splitting and Triangulation

Splitting is a phenomenon where gaslighters see things in absolutes—people are either all good or all bad—while triangulation occurs when a gaslighter talks to their victim through a third party, thus forming a triangle. With triangulation, the gaslighter intentionally starts a conflict by lying about the client's friends and family. These lies pit your client against their loved ones, further isolate them from their support network, and pull them deeper into the gaslighter's crosshairs. Meanwhile, the gaslighter sits back and gets a high from the conflict they have caused. Examples of this behavior can include:

- Telling the victim that a loved one said something negative about them (and doing so under the guise of "I think you have a right to know")
- Telling an employee that a coworker is trying to steal their job
- Telling a coworker that their boss said they are terrible at their job
- Gossiping or spreading rumors about the client's friends or family

Splitting is also common in families characterized by gaslighting, in which parents may have a "scapegoat" child that can do no right and a "golden child" that can do no wrong. The parent may switch the children's roles if they feel like one child is being disloyal or becoming their own individual. This behavior can result in lifelong conflict between siblings, particularly when the parent continues triangulating the children against each other (see chapter 5 for more information on family of origin issues).

Signs of Splitting and Triangulation

Splitting and triangulation are two common manipulation tactics that gaslighters use in their relationships. Splitting occurs when a gaslighter is very rigid in their thinking and only sees people as "all good" or "all bad," with no in between. For example, the gaslighter may switch back and forth between viewing you as the person of their dreams or lower than dirt. In these situations, it doesn't matter what you say or do—a gaslighter will treat you this way no matter what—so it is important to know that it's not your fault.

Here are some examples of splitting behaviors that your partner may engage in:

- Talking about people as either being amazing or terrible, with no middle ground
- Treating you wonderfully and then acting as if you can't do anything right
- Giving you a gift as a "reward" and then taking it back as a "punishment"
- Calling you names and then later acting kindly toward you

Describe any times you have experienced splitting behaviors from your partner.

_____

_____

_____

Splitting goes hand in hand with triangulation, in which the gaslighter acts as a messenger between you and a third party. This behavior creates drama between you and the people in your life, isolating you from loved ones and trapping you further into the gaslighter's cycle of manipulation. Your partner may be triangulating you if they engage in behaviors like these:

- Telling you that a trusted friend or relative said something negative about you
- Claiming that you "have a right to know" what someone said about you
- Talking badly to you about someone you know
- Spreading rumors about someone
- Trying to get you to dislike someone based on a confusing or unclear reason

Describe any times your partner has triangulated you.

_____

_____

_____

Weaponized Guilt and Indifference

Often, a gaslighter will punish their victim through weaponized guilt and indifference. With *weaponized guilt*, the gaslighter refuses to take responsibility for their behavior, instead blaming the victim for any problems in the relationship. They make the victim feel guilty for things that aren't their fault, causing them to blame themselves and feel powerless. The gaslighter may also intentionally ignore the victim, refusing to communicate in person, over the phone, or digitally. This behavior causes the victim to feel guilty or anxious over what they may have said or done to cause the gaslighter to act this way. The following are examples of weaponized guilt:

- A gaslighter constantly reminds their significant other of all their sacrifices in the relationship, resulting in their partner feeling guilty for any desires or needs they express.

- A parent uses guilt to manipulate their child into doing what they want by saying, "If you loved me, you would do this for me."

- A friend repeatedly brings up past favors or acts of kindness they have done, making the other person feel obligated to comply with their requests.

- An employer guilt-trips an employee for taking time off for personal reasons, implying that they are letting the team down or jeopardizing their job security.

- One sibling makes another feel guilty for pursuing their dreams or goals by saying, "You're being selfish. You should prioritize family over your ambitions."

- A partner withholds affection or sex to make their victim question what they have done wrong. When the victim asks the gaslighter why they are withholding, the gaslighter answers with "You should know" or "Of *course* you don't know. Typical."

With *weaponized indifference*, the gaslighter portrays themselves as not caring at all about what the victim does or how they feel. They consistently show disinterest, detachment, or emotional distance in response to the victim's needs or emotions. Even if the gaslighter feels a shred of emotion, they know it will hurt their victim if they act cold and indifferent. It's another way they gain power and control. The following are examples of weaponized indifference:

- One partner consistently shows little to no interest in the other's achievements, dismissing their accomplishments and making them feel insignificant.

- A parent consistently ignores their child's emotional needs, refusing to engage or offer support, leading the child to feel unimportant or unloved.

- A friend consistently fails to show up or support their friend during times of need, intentionally disregarding their feelings and creating a sense of emotional distance.

- An employer consistently ignores an employee's contributions, never acknowledging their hard work or achievements, leading the employee to feel undervalued and unappreciated.

- One family member shows indifference toward another's struggles or challenges, refusing to offer emotional support or understanding, leaving them feeling isolated and insignificant.

When clients are victimized by weaponized guilt or indifference, they may:

- Feel a persistent sense of guilt or self-blame

- Experience a constant fear of disappointing or upsetting the gaslighter

- Feel emotionally drained, invalidated, or diminished by their interactions with the gaslighter

- Notice a pattern where the gaslighter minimizes or dismisses the victim's emotions or needs

- Feel manipulated or controlled through guilt or emotional pressure

- Be afraid to express their thoughts, feelings, or desires to the gaslighter

Helping your client identify weaponized guilt and indifference in their relationship is crucial to healing. It is important to emphasize that these behaviors are not a reflection of your client's worth but, rather, a reflection of the gaslighter's pathological behavior.

Weaponized Guilt and Weaponized Indifference

When a gaslighter uses something deeply personal as a way to hurt you, it is called *weaponizing*. For example, suppose you have been diagnosed with depression. In that case, the gaslighter may tell you that your depression is the cause of all your relationship issues, or they may claim that therapy is making you "less lovable" (when the truth is that treatment is helping you feel better, be more like yourself, and have more energy to set boundaries). In this example, the gaslighter has weaponized your depression against you to make you feel guilty, known as *weaponized guilt*.

It is also common for gaslighters to use *weaponized indifference*, in which they act cold toward you, withdraw their affection, and claim they don't care about you. They may even ask you, "So why don't you just leave?" only for them to try to hoover you back into the relationship through false promises if you do attempt to leave.

What are some ways that the gaslighter has weaponized something against you?

_____

_____

_____

_____

_____

_____

_____

_____

_____

_____

_____

Projection

Projection is a defense mechanism that gaslighters use to avoid acknowledging their undesirable traits, thoughts, or behaviors. It involves attributing their feelings, thoughts, issues, or motives to their victims. For example, the gaslighter may become hostile or enraged over a minor issue and then project their anger by accusing the other person of being aggressive or having anger problems. By projecting, the gaslighter diverts attention away from themselves, creating confusion or doubt in the victim. Here are some examples of how gaslighters project:

- **Accusing others of lying:** The gaslighter consistently accuses others of being dishonest, even though they are the one frequently engaging in deceptive behaviors.

- **Blaming others for their mistakes:** The gaslighter refuses to take responsibility for their failures or errors and blames others for the consequences.

- **Criticizing others' flaws:** The gaslighter relentlessly points out and magnifies the flaws and weaknesses of others, often using these criticisms to mask their own insecurities.

- **Accusing others of being untrustworthy:** The gaslighter may constantly question the trustworthiness of others, suspecting them of betrayal or disloyalty, while the gaslighter engages in dishonest or untrustworthy behaviors.

By projecting their undesirable traits onto others, the gaslighter achieves several goals. First, projection allows the gaslighter to avoid examining their flaws, weaknesses, or insecurities by attributing them to someone else. It helps them maintain a sense of superiority or self-righteousness. Second, it allows the gaslighter to shift responsibility for their actions onto others, effectively deflecting any accountability and maintaining a position of power or control. Third, by projecting their issues onto someone else, the gaslighter is able to create confusion and make the victim question their thoughts, feelings, and experiences, which furthers the gaslighter's control.

It is essential to help clients recognize projection as a manipulation tactic and to not internalize the gaslighter's accusations or criticisms. By understanding the underlying motivations behind projection, clients can regain their confidence and trust their own judgments, allowing them to identify projection when it occurs and establish healthy boundaries in their relationships.

Projection

Projection is a manipulation tactic that gaslighters use where they will accuse *you* of engaging in a behavior *they* are doing themselves. For example, a gaslighter may accuse you of cheating even though you haven't shown any signs of infidelity—and even though they've been staying out late without explanation.

If the gaslighter is your partner, they might:

- Interrogate you when you come home late from work

- Demand to see your phone

- Accuse you of having an affair with a specific coworker or friend

- Demand that you use a tracking app on your phone to show your location

- Tell you that you can't spend time with coworkers or friends whom the gaslighter claims are interested in you

- Accuse you of being a gaslighter or narcissist

If the gaslighter is your parent, they might:

- Tell you that you are the most manipulative person they know

- Claim that you are disloyal

- Accuse you of having a favorite sibling

- Tell you that you are cheap and aren't contributing enough money to the household

- Say that practicing self-care is selfish

- Call you a gaslighter or a narcissist

Be aware that a gaslighter projects their issues onto you because they are likely profoundly insecure and have difficulties seeing the destructive nature of their behaviors. The best way to respond to these accusations is *not* to respond. Whatever comment you make can and will be used against you by the gaslighter. Remember that projection is a reflection of the gaslighter's issues, not yours. It is not personal, as much as it can feel deeply personal. Therefore, when a gaslighter makes statements like the ones above, picture them making those comments to themselves. You may start to see how much they accuse others of their own behaviors.

 Copyright © 2024 Sarkis Media LLC, *A Clinician's Guide to Gaslighting*. All rights reserved.

Invisible Armies

The term *invisible armies* describes a tactic used by gaslighters where they recruit a network of allies or supporters—who are unaware of the gaslighter's manipulative tactics or willingly complicit in their actions—to validate and reinforce the gaslighter's version of events. These allies are referred to as "invisible" because the gaslighter uses their support as ammunition against the victim while often refusing to identify who is in the "army." There is power and intimidation in numbers, especially when the gaslighter tells the victim how many people support them. Sometimes, the gaslighter will even falsely portray themselves as having a legion of supporters who think the victim is "crazy," as this allows the gaslighter to further their agenda of distorting reality, undermining others, and maintaining control. When the gaslighter refuses to name who is in their group of supporters, it makes it almost impossible for a victim to defend themselves.

The following are examples of individuals who might make up the gaslighter's invisible armies:

- **Flying monkeys:** Gaslighters may recruit friends, family members, or colleagues as flying monkeys who send messages to their victims. Flying monkeys may tell the victim how much the gaslighter misses them or guilt the victim into resuming contact. For example, in the case of a gaslighting parent, they may use comments such as "blood is thicker than water" or "honor thy mother and father." Flying monkeys can also pressure the victim into complying with the gaslighter's demands. Some flying monkeys know that they are doing the gaslighter's bidding, while others are unaware of how the gaslighter is using them.

- **Supporters in online communities:** Gaslighters may seek support in online communities or social media platforms where they find like-minded individuals who validate their perspectives and reinforce their gaslighting tactics. Gaslighters can craft an online persona or select parts of their narrative that reflect well on them. Their supporters may engage in online harassment or join campaigns to discredit or target the gaslighter's victim. In extreme cases, these supporters may engage in "swatting," where they make an untraceable phone call to emergency services stating that the gaslighter's victim is threatening others with a weapon.

- **Enablers or codependent partners:** Gaslighters often manipulate their partners or family members into enabling or codependent behavior. This behavior is often intended to help the gaslighter isolate the victim from outside support. For example, a mother-in-law may repeatedly tell her son-in-law that his family is biased against his wife and is a terrible influence on her. Enablers may unquestioningly support the gaslighter's distorted version of reality or back them out of obligation or fear.

- **Professional enablers:** In some cases, gaslighters may recruit attorneys, mental health professionals, or law enforcement personnel to be on their "side." These professionals may enable the gaslighter by dismissing the victim's concerns or reinforcing the gaslighter's narrative. They may unknowingly align with the gaslighter or willingly participate in the gaslighting process. This allows the gaslighter to use the legal system to abuse the victim through false social service calls or repeated court motions that they file. Some victims have filed for bankruptcy due to overwhelming legal costs brought about by the gaslighter using the legal system to continue contact.

As a clinician, you must help your client recognize this manipulative tactic and emphasize the importance of seeking support from trusted friends, family members, or other professionals when the client is reasonably sure the gaslighter is slandering them. Consider referring your client to an attorney if the gaslighter's invisible armies are negatively affecting your client's business or professional reputation.

Invisible Armies

Since gaslighters want to isolate you from your support network, they will say things like "Everyone thinks you're crazy" or "No one believes you." But if you ask the gaslighter who "everyone" and "no one" refers to, they usually can't give you a straight answer, which is why this manipulation tactic is called using "invisible armies" against you. The gaslighter may even claim they can't give you names because they want to protect the people supposedly talking behind your back. If they do provide you with specific names, this information is usually unverifiable. For example, they might tell you that someone said negative things about you before they passed away, which is convenient and effective because a deceased person obviously can't refute what a gaslighter has said.

The best way to respond to a gaslighter in this situation is by giving them no response. The gaslighter feeds off any emotion you give them, positive or negative. Sometimes the best response is a bland one (such as "okay" or "sure"), followed by your walking away (see chapter 8 for more information on this method, which is called "gray rock"). Be aware that giving no response or a boring response may make the gaslighter more frantic in their attempts to get your attention. You are changing the dynamics of your relationship by not feeding their ego and their need to gain control. Working toward low-contact or no-contact with a gaslighter is essential—the chances of the gaslighter changing their behavior are slim.

Copyright © 2024 Sarkis Media LLC, *A Clinician's Guide to Gaslighting*. All rights reserved.

CHAPTER 5

Vulnerability Toward Gaslighting

While no one is immune from a gaslighter's manipulation tactics, some characteristics make people more vulnerable than others. In particular, clients who are diagnosed with certain medical conditions, have suffered a recent loss, are employed in a helping profession, have a history of domestic violence, or come from a dysfunctional family of origin are often the target of gaslighters. Gaslighters will purposely seek out people with these vulnerabilities because they feel like they will be more accepting of their behavior.

In this chapter, you will learn about family of origin issues that make people more susceptible to gaslighters. You will discover how to draw a genogram, or map, of a family system to uncover patterns of behavior that lead to entrenched family dynamics. You will find information on helping your client determine their attachment style and understand how it relates to their dysfunctional relationships with gaslighters. You will also explore why trauma increases a client's vulnerability toward gaslighting. Finally, you will learn how to help your client develop a secure attachment style, making them less vulnerable to gaslighters' attempts to manipulate them.

Family of Origin Issues

When a client comes from an abusive family of origin, particularly one with emotional abuse such as gaslighting, it makes them more susceptible to being targeted by gaslighters in the future. In dysfunctional families, such as when one parent is a gaslighter and the other parent is an enabler, children may unconsciously take on specific roles to help smooth over the dysfunction in the home. However, because gaslighting parents lack consistency in their parenting, a behavior that was acceptable yesterday may result in physical abuse today. Therefore, it is not uncommon for toxic families to reverse these roles regularly. For example, a client treated as a scapegoat one day may be treated as a golden child the next. A child who experiences these radical changes in a parent's behavior and rules grows into an insecure adult who seeks approval from others and who may repeat patterns of learned dysfunctional behavior. The following are all examples of roles that your clients may identify with.

Hero

The hero is the child who is put out in public to represent the "goodness" and "worthiness" of the family. They are the child who performs well: They typically get good grades, are a star athlete, and follow all the rules. Because perfection is demanded of the hero child, they often grow up to be someone who compulsively strives for achievement and rarely takes time off to enjoy their successes. They may feel a hollow sense of accomplishment or no sense of accomplishment at all. They tend to be very hard on themselves, particularly when they think they've made a mistake.

Mascot

The mascot child may appear to be fun-loving and take on the role of the "class clown." They may use laughter to ease tensions at home. The mascot may grow up to be someone who tries to keep up the "social face" of the family. They may also appear immature due to their constant need to make jokes and act foolishly to distract outsiders from the family's dysfunction.

Lost Child

The lost child is left to their own devices and made to entertain themselves from an early age. They try to make themselves as unnoticeable as possible, keeping their head down and trying not to set the gaslighting parent off. The parents may not know where the lost child is for extended periods. No one monitors the lost child's school performance—assuming they even attend school regularly. The lost child may grow up to be an adult with passive behaviors who fears that speaking up for their needs will result in punishment.

Caretaker or Enabler

The caretaker child, also known as an enabler, becomes parentified early on in life as they become the de facto "parent" of the family. For example, they may ensure that the gaslighting parent is tucked in at night after drinking too much, and they may wake the parent up in the morning to ensure they get to work on time. It is also common for this caretaker child to be tasked with getting their siblings ready for school. Children in this role often assume a helping career in adulthood, such as a nurse or mental health professional. They frequently enter into relationships where they continue to enable another person's dysfunctional behavior.

Scapegoat

The scapegoat child is blamed for almost everything as a way to divert attention from the true source of the family's dysfunction. For example, if a parent has a bad day at work, the scapegoat is held responsible. Or if there is a conflict between siblings, the scapegoat is blamed for "instigating" the argument and punished accordingly. Even when the scapegoat is the victim of bullying, they are still viewed as the problem. Their birthday may be ignored while the other children's birthdays are celebrated. Scapegoat children often remain targets of the gaslighting parent and siblings in adulthood. They may have chronic low self-esteem, depression, and suicidality. They often believe that they are not good enough.

Golden Child

The golden child is the favored child who can do no wrong in the parent's eyes. They may be showered with gifts, praise, privileges, and other forms of positive reinforcement. While their achievements are always celebrated, any of their minor misdoings are uniformly swept under the rug. A golden child may experience guilt and shame due to the differential treatment they received from their parent. Because the golden child is put on a pedestal, they can grow into an entitled adult who fails to take responsibility for their decisions and may have difficulty apologizing for hurting others. They expect their partner to cater to their needs, and they may get irrationally angry when their partner brings up an issue.

Messages from Parents or Caregivers

If you grew up in a dysfunctional family, your parents might have used specific phrases to guilt and shame you. For example, they might have said that you were a "difficult" kid who "needed" to be punished or that your siblings were "so much easier" to raise. Your parents may still use these phrases to gain power over you today. Put a check mark by any damaging statements your parent said to you as a child that impacted your self-esteem:

☐ Why can't you be a good kid like your sibling?

☐ I should never have had you.

☐ You've brought me nothing but disappointment.

☐ After everything I've done for you, you can't do just one thing for me.

☐ You have no rights as long as you're living in my house.

☐ Don't cry, or I'll give you something to cry about.

☐ What you think happened never happened. You're confused.

☐ Your [*other family member*] would never do that. You're lying.

☐ You don't deserve nice things. You'll ruin them.

☐ You never do anything right. I'll ask your sibling to do it.

☐ I know you did it. Stop lying. Just admit it.

☐ No one cares about your feelings.

☐ Other: _____

 Copyright © 2024 Sarkis Media LLC, *A Clinician's Guide to Gaslighting*. All rights reserved.

Drawing a Genogram

Creating a genogram, which is a visual representation of family relationships and dynamics, can be an essential part of helping your client recognize family of origin patterns and issues. It allows you to explore intergenerational patterns and learn how they might impact your client's current challenges and goals. Toxic families often repeat behavior patterns across generations, resulting in trauma that gets passed down across decades. For example, many families have patterns where suicidal or self-harm behavior occurs on the same date as a beloved grandparent's death, while other families have members who repeat the same relational patterns, such as a mother and eldest daughter being distant across each generation. For victims of gaslighting, you may see a pattern of substance abuse or other dysfunctional behaviors in previous generations. You may also see a history of multiple marriages.

Clients can get closer to breaking this dysfunctional cycle by becoming aware of these generational patterns. It is often not until you show a client their genogram that they realize what they are experiencing was encoded into the family long ago. By understanding the family context, you can help your client discover how their family experiences have shaped their beliefs and behaviors today, allowing you to identify potential strengths, vulnerabilities, and areas for growth. Genograms can also assist you by reminding you of family members' names and relationships.

When creating a genogram, you should include lines signifying types of relationships (e.g., enmeshed, close, conflicted, cut off), dates of marriages and divorces, medical diagnoses, deaths in the family (including the cause of death and age at the time of death), and dates of any other significant events.

The following is an example of a genogram key. Note that this is not meant to be an exhaustive list of possible identities or types of relationships, just a starting point. The client can modify or add symbols in their genogram to best represent themselves and their family.

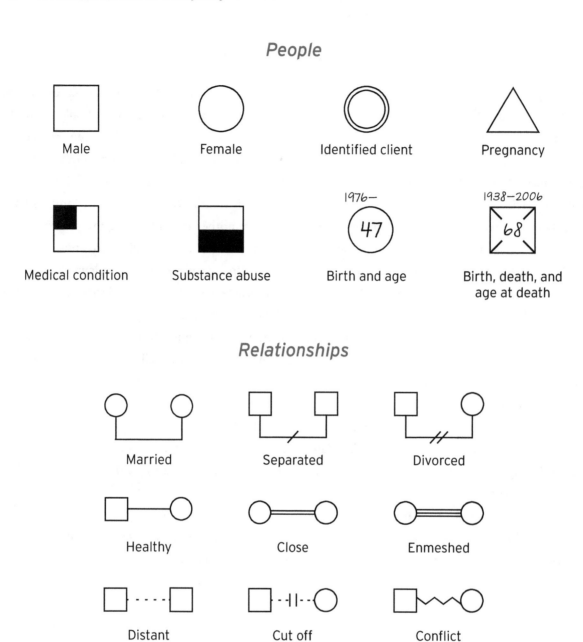

To understand the significance of the genogram in identifying family patterns, let's explore the hypothetical story of a 32-year-old client named Sarah. Sarah's parents, Mark and Vicky, divorced when Sarah was five years old and both remarried several years later. Mark is now married to Wafa, and they have a 21-year-old daughter named Rania. Mark is an alcoholic and has been in recovery for five years. Sarah and Mark often get into yelling matches whenever they interact, and Sarah rarely speaks to Rania because, as she states, she doesn't "have anything in common with her." Vicky is now married to Jorge, and they have an 18-year-old daughter named Isabel. Jorge and Isabel share a love of fishing, and they are close. As for Sarah, she is married to John, and they have two children, Michael, 10, and Zoe, 7. However, Sarah and John recently separated due to what Sarah describes as "growing apart."

The following genogram provides valuable information about Sarah's family dynamics and relationships. It shows the intricacies of her family, including disrupted relationships, which may have influenced Sarah's experiences and her perceptions of relationships and family. For example, Sarah's family has a pattern of divorce and remarriage, which may indicate a cycle of relationship difficulties or challenges in maintaining long-term partnerships. Additionally, her genogram helps identify potential sources of support or conflict within the family system. For instance, Sarah's relationships with her half-siblings and stepparents may influence her sense of belonging and emotional well-being.

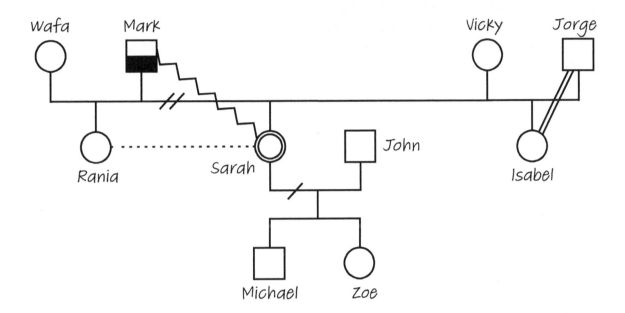

As Sarah's example illustrates, genograms are a powerful tool for uncovering hidden patterns, highlighting areas of resilience, and facilitating a deeper understanding of the client's story. It aids the therapeutic process by providing a framework for exploring family dynamics, fostering insight, and promoting healing and growth.

After you work with your client to create a genogram, review their work and emphasize that while genetics and family patterns play a vital role in our health and behavior, they are not destiny. Uncovering these patterns decreases the chances that your client will continue repeating them. Let your client know they always have free will and the choice to change and break the family cycle.

Draw Your Genogram

Gaslighting and other forms of family dysfunction are often intergenerational, meaning that they are inadvertently passed down from one generation to the next. To help you better understand the life experiences that may have made you more susceptible to gaslighting, consider which of your family members have engaged in manipulative or toxic behaviors that may have made you question your reality and doubt yourself. Create a list of these individuals (this might include your parents, siblings, grandparents, aunts, uncles, cousins, and so forth) and describe their gaslighting behaviors.

_____

_____

_____

_____

_____

_____

_____

_____

_____

_____

_____

_____

_____

_____

_____

_____

_____

_____

_____

Copyright © 2024 Sarkis Media LLC, *A Clinician's Guide to Gaslighting.* All rights reserved.

When you're done, use this information to help you create a genogram, a graphical representation of the relationships in your family. Your genogram should include dates of marriages, divorces, and deaths in the family, as well as medical diagnoses, causes of death, ages at the time of death, and any other information you feel is important to include. The following key offers symbols you can use to represent the different people, relationships, and life events in your family. Note that this is not meant to be an exhaustive list of all the possibilities—you can also modify the symbols or add your own to best represent yourself and your family.

Genogram Key

People

Male   Female   Identified client   Pregnancy

Medical condition   Substance abuse   Birth and age   Birth, death, and age at death

Relationships

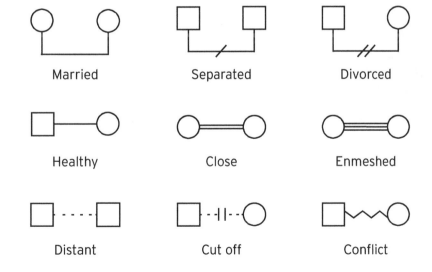

Married   Separated   Divorced

Healthy   Close   Enmeshed

Distant   Cut off   Conflict

Copyright © 2024 Sarkis Media LLC, *A Clinician's Guide to Gaslighting*. All rights reserved.

Your Genogram

Copyright © 2024 Sarkis Media LLC, *A Clinician's Guide to Gaslighting*. All rights reserved.

Do You Have Fleas?

Gaslighting parents use manipulation to get power and control over their children. If you grew up in a gaslighting family, your parent may have frequently manipulated and pitted you against your siblings. Your parent may even have had a "golden child" who could do no wrong and a "scapegoat child" who could do no right, with these roles potentially switching based on how each child could best serve the parent at that moment. Your parent may also have demanded loyalty but rarely showed it in return. They may have purposefully embarrassed you in front of your friends or stonewalled you and refused to talk to you when you stood up for yourself or refused to enable them.

If you grew up around a gaslighting parent, you likely started using some of their behaviors as a way to survive. For example, if your parent never gave you lunch money as a child, you may have been forced into manipulative tactics at school just to get fed. As an adult, you may repeat these same patterns and use gaslighting behaviors in your relationships without realizing it. In other words, you picked up "fleas" from your parent. Fleas are gaslighting behaviors that you acquired from your parent through no fault of your own. It comes from the saying, "If you lie down with a dog, you get up with fleas."

It's important to remember that you were a child and didn't have a choice in your home environment. You were doing the best you could in a very difficult situation. In therapy, you can talk to a trusted mental health professional about how your past experiences may have shaped who you are today. Therapy is hard work, but you get out of it what you put into it—once you realize you have behaviors you want to change, there is a good chance that you will be successful in making those changes.

What Does a Healthy Family Look Like?

If you grew up in a gaslighting family, you might be well-versed in chaos and dysfunction but not in healthy relationship dynamics. Identifying dysfunction in your family and learning what makes up a healthy family is essential. Although many people think that a healthy family is one in which there is an absence of arguing, the reality is that conflict is an unavoidable aspect of all relationships. The difference in a healthy family, though, is that family members talk through these disagreements with mutual respect, kindness, and love. If one person has hurt another, they take ownership of it and apologize, without conditions and with a clear promise of how they will change their behavior in the future.

The following are all qualities of an emotionally healthy family:

- People can express their feelings and disagree with each other while feeling safe and treating each other with respect.

- Family members are free from addiction or in recovery.

- People respect each other's privacy and boundaries, including physical space.

- Parents provide guidance and support to their children.

- All people are treated with respect and kindness.

- Everyone has the right to say no at any time.

- Everyone demonstrates care, love, and affection toward each other.

- Family members spend quality time together and make time for fun activities together.

- Equality and fairness are encouraged.

- People apologize when someone's feelings are hurt.

- Concerns are brought up without fear of retribution or punishment.

- Communication is open and honest.

- Family members support each other's personal growth.

- Everyone appreciates each other's unique abilities and cultural backgrounds.

- Family members participate equally in family chores (with age and developmental level being taken into consideration).

- Adults model appropriate behavior for children.

    Copyright © 2024 Sarkis Media LLC, *A Clinician's Guide to Gaslighting*. All rights reserved.

Previous Trauma

In addition to family of origin issues, a history of trauma can make your client more vulnerable to gaslighting. This trauma may be related to other experiences of emotional abuse or domestic violence, or it may be unrelated to their current gaslighting experience. Any trauma increases susceptibility to gaslighting because it can profoundly impact an individual's sense of self and interfere with their ability to trust their perceptions. Here's how trauma can contribute to this vulnerability:

- **Diminished self-esteem:** Trauma often erodes an individual's self-worth and leads them to internalize negative beliefs about themselves. Gaslighters take advantage of this by silencing, belittling, or ridiculing their victims—further diminishing their self-esteem and making them rely more on the gaslighter for validation and guidance.

- **Distorted perception of reality:** Trauma can disrupt an individual's ability to perceive and interpret events accurately. Memories may become fragmented, emotions may be overwhelming, and dissociation or numbing may occur as a coping mechanism. Gaslighters exploit these vulnerabilities by dismissing the victim's emotions or experiences, making them further question their sense of reality.

- **Hypervigilance and self-doubt:** Trauma leads to hypervigilance—a heightened awareness and sensitivity to potential threats. Gaslighters take advantage of this heightened state by creating an environment of constant uncertainty and doubt. The gaslighter may use subtle manipulation tactics, such as contradicting the victim's account of events or rewriting history, causing the victim to question their memory and judgment.

- **Dependency and isolation:** Trauma can create a sense of dependency on others for safety and security. Gaslighters often exploit this dependency by isolating the victim from their support networks, making them more reliant on the gaslighter for validation and emotional stability. This isolation further limits the victim's ability to seek validation from others and reinforces the gaslighter's control over their reality.

- **Reenactment of past abuse:** Trauma can leave individuals more vulnerable to reenacting abusive dynamics from their past. Someone with a history of trauma may inadvertently attract or be attracted to gaslighters who replicate patterns of emotional abuse or manipulation they have previously experienced. The gaslighter may sense this vulnerability and exploit it to gain power and control over the victim.

As a therapist, you must help your client unpack their traumatic experiences at their own pace without pressuring them to move too quickly. When working with clients who have experienced trauma through gaslighting and other forms of emotional abuse, remember the following:

- Take time to develop rapport with your client before discussing their history of trauma. Approaching the trauma too quickly and on your terms, instead of the client's, can cause them to shut down and result in more harm.

- Often, survivors of abuse have no choice but to leave without loved ones, such as siblings, children, or pets. If your client left an abusive situation but could not take their loved ones, they may be experiencing survivor's guilt. It is crucial to help your client process these feelings and associated grief at their own pace.

- If you also have a history of trauma, you may experience flashbacks, dissociation, or countertransference. Make sure to seek your own therapy when working with traumatized clients. See chapter 13 for more information on vicarious trauma.

- Keep your self-disclosure in check. If you went through a similar experience as your client, you might be tempted to share that experience to help them feel less alone. However, your client has been through a traumatic experience, and their brain may start processing your trauma as their own. You also risk having a codependent client enact caretaking behaviors with you.

- Never underestimate the power of sharing space with someone and listening to their story. You are working with a client who likely hasn't shared their experiences with anyone else. Just being there as a listener can be enough.

- Emotional abuse, such as gaslighting, can be just as damaging, if not more, than physical abuse.

For more information on helping clients work through past trauma, see chapter 7.

Attachment Style

Attachment style is the affectional tie we have to specific people (D'Arienzo et al., 2019). Attachment styles are crucial in shaping how individuals form and maintain relationships with others. The four main attachment styles are secure, anxious, avoidant, and disorganized, with the latter three reflecting what is known as insecure attachment. Your client's attachment style is rooted in their family of origin, and if your client was emotionally abused when growing up, they might struggle with an insecure attachment style today. Not only can these unresolved attachment issues be passed down to future generations, but it also makes a difference in how clients navigate their relationship with a gaslighter. For example, a client may exhibit secure attachment in healthy relationships but lean toward anxious attachment in the presence of a gaslighter.

By learning your client's primary attachment style, you gain a deeper understanding of the influence of the trauma bond on the client's ability to separate from a gaslighter. It can also provide additional information about their ability to heal after ending a relationship with a gaslighter. For example, clients with an anxious attachment style will likely have more intense grief experiences after cutting off contact (Heshmati et al., 2022). The following paragraphs describe how each attachment style can relate to vulnerability toward gaslighting.

Secure Attachment

Individuals with a secure attachment style likely grew up with caregivers who were stable and met their needs. As adults, these individuals typically have a favorable view of themselves and others. They feel comfortable with emotional intimacy and independence, trust their partners, and expect trust in return. They tend to practice proactive self-care, can emotionally "recalibrate," and can communicate issues directly yet respectfully. They have a healthy sense of self-worth and are likelier to have healthy boundaries. This secure base helps protect them from gaslighting, as they have a solid foundation of self-assurance and are less likely to doubt their perceptions or accept manipulative narratives. Securely attached clients may be able to spot gaslighting behaviors early on and not engage in a relationship with someone they suspect is emotionally unhealthy.

Anxious Attachment

Individuals with an anxious attachment style were raised by caregivers who were unpredictable or intrusive. As adults, they often seek a high level of closeness and validation from their partners. They also worry about abandonment, fear rejection, and frequently seek reassurance. They may experience separation anxiety and be preoccupied with others' feelings while ignoring their own. They may not directly address concerns due to a fear of rejection. These insecurities and fears can make them more vulnerable to gaslighting. Furthermore, individuals with an anxious attachment style may be more inclined to question their thoughts and feelings, which gaslighters will exploit by encouraging their self-doubt and manipulating reality.

Avoidant Attachment

Individuals with an avoidant (also called dismissive) attachment style grew up with caregivers who were distant and unresponsive to their needs. As adults, they tend to prize independence and self-reliance. They have difficulty forming close emotional connections and prefer to maintain distance in relationships, given that they may view a relationship as a threat to their independence. Avoidantly attached individuals often struggle with intimacy and may dismiss their own or others' emotions. This detachment and emotional distancing can make them more susceptible to gaslighting, as they may be less attuned to their own needs and more willing to dismiss or doubt their own experiences.

Disorganized Attachment

Individuals with a disorganized attachment style often grew up with caregivers who were unpredictable or abusive. They may have also experienced other forms of trauma or abusive relationships, leading to unresolved emotional conflicts. As adults, these individuals display inconsistent and contradictory behaviors in their relationships. For example, they may crave emotional intimacy but also fear becoming engulfed by it. They also tend to lack coping skills, exhibit difficulties meeting their own needs, and experience frequent dissociation. They may have difficulty trusting others and asking for help. Disorganized attachment can enhance vulnerability to gaslighting, as these individuals have difficulty establishing a coherent sense of self and struggle with trusting their perceptions. Gaslighters may exploit their emotional turmoil and confusion, further destabilizing their sense of reality.

As a client with an insecure attachment style moves toward secure attachment, the gaslighter may become less interested in interacting with them, or they may quickly ramp up their manipulative behavior to ensure their narcissistic supply continues. These responses from the gaslighter may trigger your client toward insecure attachment again. It's important to emphasize to your client that they are still progressing and healing, even if they feel they have regressed into a previous insecure attachment style. Progress is a jagged climb with highs and lows, not a continual perfect incline, yet it is always moving forward.

Working with a client to understand their attachment style can provide them with insights into vulnerabilities that gaslighters may have exploited. Therapeutic interventions that focus on developing secure attachment, promoting self-esteem, and enhancing emotional resilience can help clients overcome the effects of insecure attachment, move toward secure attachment, and protect themselves from gaslighting.

Discover Your Attachment Style

A person's attachment style reflects how they relate to others in a relationship. There are four main attachment styles: secure, anxious, avoidant, and disorganized. Many people have a primary attachment style that shows up in most or all of their relationships, although they may also have characteristics of other styles. To understand your own attachment style, read through the following statements and put a check mark by any you identify with.

☐   1.   When my partner hasn't contacted me, I get anxious.

☐   2.   Getting into a relationship means I lose my independence.

☐   3.   Having a relationship end is one of my major fears.

☐   4.   I need a lot of space when I get emotionally close to someone.

☐   5.   I call or text a lot when my partner is out.

☐   6.   I prefer long-distance relationships so I can have my freedom.

☐   7.   I have been told I am "needy" or "clingy" in relationships.

☐   8.   I have been told I am "distant" or "aloof" in relationships.

☐   9.   I will do whatever it takes to keep a relationship going.

☐   10.   I would be okay with never having a relationship again.

To obtain a total score, tally the number of items you marked in each section:

Odd-numbered items: _____   Even-numbered items: _____

If you checked off more odd-numbered items, you might have an **anxious** attachment style. The following characteristics may be true for you:

- Your caregivers were unpredictable or smothering.

- Losing a relationship is one of your worst fears.

- You feel anxious when separated from your partner for even short periods.

- You consider others' feelings more than your own.

- You need closeness and intimacy to feel comfortable.

- You tend to get passive-aggressive toward your partner when you are upset.

- You don't state your needs, wants, and feelings due to fears of rejection.

Copyright © 2024 Sarkis Media LLC, *A Clinician's Guide to Gaslighting*. All rights reserved.

If you checked off more even-numbered items, you might have an **avoidant** attachment style, meaning the following may be true for you:

- Your caregivers were distant and unresponsive to your needs.

- You take great pride in your ability to be independent and self-reliant.

- You view a relationship as a possible threat to your independence.

- You may appear aloof and distant to others.

- You tend to be uncomfortable with emotional intimacy.

- You can be rigid, critical, or intolerant of others.

- You gravitate toward long-distance relationships.

If you checked off a mix of odd and even numbers, you might have a **disorganized** attachment style. In this case, the following may be true for you:

- Your caregivers were unpredictable and abusive.

- You have great difficulty coping with adversity.

- You are not sure what your needs and wants are in a relationship.

- You may dissociate and detach from your feelings.

- You have difficulty asking for help and trusting others.

- You want emotional intimacy with another person, but it also terrifies you.

- You push partners away but then feel abandoned and pursue them.

If you checked off fewer than five items total, you might have a **secure** attachment style. You might resonate with the following experiences:

- Your caregivers were emotionally stable and met your needs.

- You feel comfortable with emotional intimacy.

- You feel the goal of a relationship is interdependence, not dependence.

- You proactively practice daily self-care.

- You notice when you are emotionally "off" and can get yourself back on track.

- You directly communicate your needs, wants, and feelings.

Consider sharing your results with your mental health professional so you can explore together how your primary attachment style may be affecting your relationships and well-being.

 Copyright © 2024 Sarkis Media LLC, *A Clinician's Guide to Gaslighting*. All rights reserved.

How Your Attachment Style
Impacts Your Relationships

Your attachment style is formed in your relationships with your caregivers in childhood, but it goes on to affect the way you relate with other people in your life. If you were raised by gaslighters or are in a current relationship with a gaslighter, you might have an anxious, avoidant, or disorganized attachment style. If you were raised by emotionally stable, attentive caregivers (or if you have worked to overcome the challenges of your initial attachment style), you may have a secure attachment style instead. The following paragraphs describe how the different styles typically affect our relationships.

In **secure** attachment, partners are interdependent. Each person has their own interests, but they also form a collective "we." If the relationship ends, a person with secure attachment may be upset. Still, they know they learned a lot from the relationship and will be able to move on.

In **anxious** attachment, a person may become preoccupied with thoughts of their partner leaving them. They may consent to whatever their partner wants to preserve the relationship, even when it goes against their own needs and desires. A person with anxious attachment may see the dissolution of a relationship as something to be avoided at all costs.

In **avoidant** attachment, independence is emphasized to the point where there is a lack of emotional attachment to a partner. Someone with avoidant attachment may see vulnerability and time spent with their partner as a threat to their independence. They may prefer long-distance relationships as a way to maintain emotional distance as well.

In **disorganized** attachment, there are features of both anxious attachment and avoidant attachment. A person may want their partner to be emotionally closer to them but fear such intimacy at the same time because it makes them feel vulnerable to being hurt. As a result, they may alternate between pushing their partner away and pursuing them again.

Copyright © 2024 Sarkis Media LLC, *A Clinician's Guide to Gaslighting*. All rights reserved.

Working Toward Secure Attachment

If your client exhibits anxious, avoidant, or disorganized attachment in their relationships, you will want to discuss how to move toward a secure attachment style. To begin, review your client's answers to the previous attachment style quiz, then explore the origins of this attachment style. Helpful information to ask about includes:

- What was the composition of their family of origin? What were their parents' attachment styles like? (Refer back to the genogram exercise earlier in this chapter.)

- How did their parents respond to their needs? Were they distant, unpredictable, smothering, or nurturing?

- How has gaslighting or other emotionally abusive behaviors impacted their attachment style?

- Are there differences in their attachment styles across different relationships? In what relationships do they experience a more secure attachment style? What is it about these relationships that makes for healthier interactions?

- What would your client like their relationships to look like?

It is helpful to provide your client with information about what secure attachment looks like within a relationship. As therapists, we tend to provide clients with examples of unhealthy relationships, but we don't always explain what is considered to be an emotionally healthy relationship. The following handout will help you to do so. Reinforce that people can change their attachment style by engaging in introspection; identifying problematic behaviors in potential partners, friends, and family members; and focusing on forming healthier relationships.

Signs of Secure Attachment

When you have a secure attachment style:

- Your relationship is part of your life but isn't your whole life.

- You are willing to take the emotional risk of loving someone even though you know there aren't any guarantees it will work out.

- You encourage your partner to pursue their own interests.

- You speak up for what you want and need in a relationship.

- You feel free to be yourself, even if it means a relationship might end.

- You connect with your partner when you aren't together, but you are both comfortable with the frequency of contact.

- You and your partner can meet each other halfway, and you don't feel like you are compromising your values and beliefs in the process.

- You end a relationship if your wants and needs are consistently unmet.

- You are okay knowing that relationships change over time and that people may grow apart or have different needs and wants.

- You do kind things for your partner without expecting anything in return.

- You address issues with your partner assertively yet kindly.

- You don't tolerate abuse of any kind from your partner.

- You are okay with your partner going out with their friends and even appreciate the time alone.

- You know you'll be okay if your relationship ends.

- You express your wants and needs to your partner without guilt or shame.

- You take a step back when stressed and take time for self-care.

- You can identify other securely attached people and tend to be attracted to them.

- You encourage your children to gain developmentally appropriate independence.

Although a secure attachment style may not come naturally to you, you can develop secure attachment by engaging in self-reflection and working through your trauma in therapy. Consider talking with your mental health professional about how you can work toward developing a secure attachment style.

Copyright © 2024 Sarkis Media LLC, *A Clinician's Guide to Gaslighting*. All rights reserved.

CHAPTER 6

The Trauma Bond

It is difficult for victims of gaslighting and other forms of abuse to leave those relationships. While it may seem deceptively simple to an outsider—someone treats you poorly, so you leave—this point of view does not consider the impact of the trauma bond. The trauma bond reflects the attachment that a victim forms with their abuser. This occurs when a victim is caught in a cycle of abuse that oscillates between periods of emotional abuse and brief moments of positive reinforcement and kindness. Through each cycle, the abuser and victim form a more intense attachment, particularly if the victim has strong empathy for the abuser (Effiong et al., 2022).

In this chapter, you will learn about the trauma bond and why it is so difficult for victims of gaslighting to go no-contact or low-contact with their abuser. You will also explore how cognitive distortions can result from and contribute to the trauma bond. To help clients break free, you'll explore how to help them replace their inner critic with a loving, compassionate voice. You'll also discover how codependency can continue a "needing to be needed" cycle. Finally, you'll be guided through helping clients go no-contact or low-contact with their gaslighter, including handling any guilt or shame they may experience after cutting off contact with a gaslighting parent.

The Trauma Bond

As you learned in chapter 4, toxic relationships are characterized by a three-phase cycle of abuse—idealization, devaluation, and discarding—sometimes followed by a hoovering phase. This cycle traps victims into what is known as the trauma bond, in which they develop feelings of sympathy, love, and connection to the person who is gaslighting them. They may cover up or make excuses for their abuser's behavior, minimize the severity of the abuse, and defend their abuser. Victims may also become emotionally dependent on their abuser and feel a strong need for their approval or validation, even when the relationship is unhealthy or harmful.

Part of the reason the trauma bond is so strong is because of the power of intermittent reinforcement. The abuser provides the victim with unpredictable and intermittent acts of seeming kindness, love, and validation, which causes the victim to cling to the belief that things will improve. Over time, the brain adapts to this cycle, reinforcing the emotional connection to the abuser and making it even more challenging to break free. At the biochemical level, intermittent reinforcement activates the same reward circuits associated with addiction, which triggers the release of dopamine, a neurotransmitter associated with pleasure and motivation, as well as endorphins and oxytocin. As a result, victims can become emotionally "addicted" to their abusers, experiencing withdrawal-like symptoms when attempting to sever ties or maintain no-contact.

The consequences of the trauma bond can be profound and long-lasting. Victims may experience confusion, self-blame, and a distorted perception of reality. They may struggle with low self-esteem, weak personal boundaries, and a sense of powerlessness. The trauma bond can also contribute to the victim's reluctance to leave the abusive relationship, as they may fear the unknown, feel guilt or shame about leaving the relationship, or believe they are unable to survive without their abuser.

Understanding the trauma bond is crucial in supporting clients who have experienced gaslighting and other forms of abuse. You can help clients recognize the signs of trauma bonding, validate their experiences, and provide a safe space to explore the complexities of their emotions. Therapeutic interventions focus on rebuilding self-esteem, establishing healthy boundaries, and developing alternative coping strategies to break the cycle of abuse and gradually overcome the trauma bond. It is also helpful to explain the addictive power of intermittent reinforcement—emphasizing that the trauma bond is something our brains automatically do—as this can help reduce your client's guilt and shame.

Understanding the Trauma Bond

You may have noticed that your relationship with a gaslighter is like a rollercoaster. It is never steady—there are always extreme highs and lows—and things never genuinely feel calm. Sometimes the gaslighter criticizes and berates you, leaving you to wonder what you did wrong, while other times, they seem kind and even loving toward you, especially when they think you might cut off contact with them. You are always wondering when the next explosion is going to happen.

If so, you may be experiencing what is known as the *trauma bond*, which is the particular type of emotional attachment that people often develop with the very person who is harming them. The trauma bond is powerful because it causes biochemical changes to your brain that can make you addicted to the relationship. During the idealization phase of the relationship, your brain produces increased amounts of dopamine (the "feel-good" neurotransmitter) and oxytocin (the "cuddle" hormone). But when your relationship goes into the devaluation phase, you produce more cortisol and adrenaline (stress hormones). When the gaslighter returns to giving you positive attention and affection, you're rewarded with another rush of dopamine and oxytocin, thus reinforcing the cycle.

The more your relationship loops around this cycle, the more your brain becomes dependent on those chemicals. It gets addicted to the ups and downs of the relationship. Therefore, when you try to leave a gaslighting relationship, it can feel like you are experiencing drug withdrawal. To successfully move on, your brain must learn how to function again without the accompanying rush of these chemicals. Fortunately, the more distance you put between you and the gaslighter, the more your brain recovers from this vicious cycle.

Copyright © 2024 Sarkis Media LLC, *A Clinician's Guide to Gaslighting*. All rights reserved.

Cognitive Distortions

Cognitive distortions are part of the self-talk that constantly runs through our minds. Often, they are the brain's way of tormenting us into believing that the worst events will befall us and that others are thinking negatively about us. Your client most likely has been experiencing an influx of cognitive distortions after absorbing the destructive lies the gaslighter has told them. Here are some common cognitive distortions seen in these situations:

- **Minimization:** Victims may downplay or dismiss the severity of the abuse they have experienced. They may convince themselves that the gaslighter's actions are not that harmful or that they are overreacting—thus denying the reality of the situation. You will want to educate your client on the trauma bond and explain how the gaslighter's cycle of abuse and fear—interspersed with love bombing, kindness, and affection—can result in deep dependency that makes victims more likely to overlook the gaslighter's abusive behavior.

- **Self-blame:** Clients often internalize the gaslighter's messages and blame themselves for the abuse. They may believe they deserve mistreatment or are somehow responsible for the gaslighter's behavior, even though it is entirely the gaslighter's choice to engage in abusive tactics. It is important to help your client understand that gaslighting is never the victim's fault. It is a deliberate and manipulative tactic employed by the gaslighter.

- **All-or-nothing thinking:** Victims of gaslighting may engage in black-and-white thinking and struggle to acknowledge the gray areas and complexities of the situation. For example, they may idealize the image of the gaslighter while demonizing themselves. Help your client identify the "middle ground" where people aren't purely good or bad but may behave in ways detrimental to our well-being.

- **Emotional reasoning:** Clients may rely solely on their emotions as evidence of truth, disregarding objective facts or evidence. For example, if they feel guilty, they use these feelings as facts and automatically assume they did something wrong or are at fault—even though the gaslighter is truly to blame. Discuss the difference between feelings and facts with your client and explain that just because we feel an emotion doesn't make it true. Instead, encourage your client to check the objective facts of the situation.

- **Overgeneralization:** Clients may draw sweeping conclusions based on isolated incidents of abuse. They might believe that because the gaslighter mistreated them, they are inherently unworthy or deserving of mistreatment in all areas of life. By thinking they are deserving of injustice, they have given the gaslighter an immense amount of power. Challenge your client to provide evidence that their belief in being undeserving extends past this relationship.

- **Fortune-telling:** Clients may engage in fortune-telling by predicting that their future will consist of another gaslighting relationship or that they will be unable to move on and create a new path forward. The gaslighter took options away from your client, so they understandably may envision a bleak future. Work with your client in separating fact from speculation. What does your client know for sure, and what is speculation?

- **Should statements:** Victims of gaslighting may state that they should have left the relationship long ago or should be moving on more quickly. These should statements can result in guilt and shame and cause your client to feel paralyzed by moral imperatives. To help your client move on, have them substitute their should statements with phrases like "would prefer" or "would like to." This change allows for more freedom of action and influence over their life changes.

- **Labeling:** Clients may give negative labels to themselves or others, especially if they were in a relationship where they were constantly criticized and told they weren't good enough. Your client may call themselves an "idiot" when they spill their coffee or label a friend as "lazy" because they are taking a day off for self-care. These negative labels generalize who someone is, instead of looking at a specific behavior. Help your client identify these negative labels and replace them with an objective statement about their or another's behavior, such as "I spilled my coffee" or "My friend needs some down time."

Addressing these cognitive distortions is a crucial aspect of therapy for victims of gaslighting who have experienced a trauma bond. As clients learn to challenge and reframe these distorted beliefs, they develop more accurate and balanced thinking patterns—and you are supporting their healing journey and empowering them to regain control over their lives.

Cognitive Distortions

When you have a gaslighter in your life, you are more likely to experience cognitive distortions. These are unhelpful thoughts your brain creates, especially when you are under stress or facing challenges. Although cognitive distortions can feel like truths, they are biased ways of thinking that often don't reflect reality. You can think of it as the voice of your inner critic. See if any of your internal dialogue falls into one or more of these categories:

- **Minimizing:** You act as if a big issue is of little importance.

    EXAMPLE: "He drinks ten beers a night, so what? He doesn't have a problem."

- **Self-blame:** You internalize toxic messages you received from someone and believe you are at fault.

    EXAMPLE: "He said I'm terrible at relationships. I guess I deserve to be alone."

- **All-or-nothing thinking:** You see situations or people as either all good or all bad—there is no in between.

    EXAMPLE: "I texted her this morning and she hasn't texted me back. I'm done with her."

- **Emotional reasoning:** You mistake emotions for facts.

    EXAMPLE: "I feel guilty, so I must have done something wrong in my relationship."

- **Overgeneralization:** You make broad conclusions about one specific event by generalizing it to all future events.

    EXAMPLE: "She couldn't go with me to the concert; I have no friends."

- **Fortune-telling:** You predict that things will turn out the worst possible way.

    Example: "I know this presentation at work will go terribly, and I will get fired."

- **Should statements:** You think in terms of *shoulds*, *oughts*, or *musts*—never giving yourself a break and always telling yourself that you must do a certain task if you are a "good" person.

    EXAMPLE: "I should call my friend. I'm really tired, but a good friend would call now."

- **Labeling:** You use a negative label to define your entire personality based on an isolated event.

    EXAMPLE: "I can't believe she turned me down. I am such a loser."

 Copyright © 2024 Sarkis Media LLC, *A Clinician's Guide to Gaslighting*. All rights reserved.

Calming the Inner Critic and Developing a Loving Inner Voice

A crucial part of combating cognitive distortions involves helping your client replace their inner critic with a loving inner voice. Remember that the gaslighter has manipulated your client and told them many lies to make them question their thoughts, opinions, and feelings. They have told your client that they are crazy, weak, stupid, and incapable of surviving independently. Over time, your client has unknowingly internalized these comments, which they now repeat to themselves. As a result, they have come to doubt themselves and their ability to function in the world without the gaslighter, thus reinforcing the trauma bond.

To help your client heal from this gaslighting and break free from the trauma bond, you must teach them to identify when they are using their critical inner voice. For example, it may be that their inner critic is more prone to show up at work or when the client is socializing. Either way, have your client write down their inner critic's comments as they happen in real time. Your client will become more aware of the frequency of their negative and critical comments—which is usually more often than they would have expected. When your client stays in the here and now while processing their inner critic's words, they more accurately record how they are critiquing themselves throughout the day.

In addition, have your client identify where they may have heard those comments in the past. Does this inner critic represent the voice of a parent, teacher, significant other, or all of the above? This identification is essential because some unresolved issues or trauma may need to be processed in session. There may be some lasting damage from hypercritical people in your client's life, and those relationships should be addressed.

Finally, have your client write down comments from a loving inner voice that can replace the critical ones. This inner voice is kind and loving but also sets healthy boundaries. Loving inner voice comments include:

- You're doing great.
- You are doing the best you can, and that is enough.
- You've done enough work for today. Time for some rest.
- You are always enough.

If your client is having difficulty creating a loving inner voice, consider recommending that they think of a fictional character, mentor, or role model that they would have chosen as a parent for themselves. If your client has a good relationship with their children, have them speak to themselves as they would speak to their children. Let them know that cultivating a loving inner voice can take a while, especially if they grew up with a gaslighting parent. But progress is progress, even if it feels small at the time.

Replace Your Inner Critic with a Loving Inner Voice

We all have an inner voice that makes comments throughout the day. Many times, those comments are unkind or downright cruel. If you have been in a relationship with a gaslighter, you probably hear your inner critic more frequently and intensely. You may even hear those unkind comments as if they are being said in the gaslighter's voice.

What negative comments has your inner critic told you this week?

_____

_____

_____

_____

Does the voice of your inner critic remind you of anyone you know?

_____

_____

Now it's time to replace that critical voice with a loving one. If you aren't sure who to model your loving voice after, think of a fictional character you would have selected as a good parent. Or speak to yourself the same way you would to your children or a dear friend. Who is someone that could serve as your loving inner voice?

_____

What would this loving inner voice say to you instead?

_____

_____

_____

_____

The more you practice using your loving inner voice, the more likely you will be to automatically start using it.

Codependency

Relationships characterized by the trauma bond have an element of codependency in that the victim will often judge themselves harshly and minimize the gaslighter's dysfunctional behavior. Instead of realizing that the gaslighter is to blame, the victim will take responsibility for their partner's abusive behavior and apologize for "setting them off," thus enabling the gaslighter to continue the cycle of destruction.

This dynamic represents the core nature of codependency, which is often described as "setting yourself on fire to keep another person warm." Because codependent people need to be needed, they deny their needs to please others. They take responsibility for other people's behavior and put others' well-being before their own. To do so, a codependent person will push down their feelings so they don't "take up space" or upset the other person. In turn, it is common for codependent people to sublimate anger and fear into passive-aggressive behavior. This can include:

- Responding angrily with "I'm fine" when someone asks how they are doing
- Purposefully burning someone's dinner or "forgetting" to tell them a package arrived for them
- Giving backhanded compliments
- Sabotaging others
- Taking on the role of a martyr and complaining about never being appreciated

Therefore, when working through the trauma bond, consider whether some of your client's behaviors have possibly enabled the gaslighter. It doesn't mean your client "caused" the gaslighting behavior but, instead, that your client may not have asserted themselves because they feared being threatened, harassed, or demeaned. As a result of the trauma bond, they may also feel a sense of loyalty to their abuser. Your client may also not have protected their children from the gaslighter, resulting in guilt and shame.

Discussing the concept of codependency with your client is essential, including how it perpetuates learned helplessness and the trauma bond. The following are some signs that your client may be exhibiting codependent behaviors:

- They believe their partner's needs are more important than their own.
- They have missed important events because their partner guilted or shamed them into not going.
- They have stopped speaking to certain family members and friends because of their partner.
- They make up excuses for their partner's abusive behavior.
- They have financially supported their partner to the point where it has hurt their credit or savings.
- They have been physically and emotionally abused but remain in the relationship.
- They often return to unhealthy relationships.

- They ask for your approval when making decisions.

- They are focused on "working things out" instead of leaving a dysfunctional relationship.

- They have procured drugs or other addictive substances for a family member or partner.

Although there is some controversy surrounding the term *codependence*, nothing is healthy about being caught in the cycle of abuse that characterizes gaslighting relationships. The problem is not just about depending on another person; it's about being caught in a destructive relationship where clients are entirely cut off from their support network and at risk of escalating violence and trauma. Helping clients escape this cycle requires working with them to build an identity separate from the gaslighter.

What Is Codependency?

Codependency happens when you put someone else's needs before your own. It might be appropriate in certain circumstances to temporarily prioritize others' needs, such as when your children's safety is threatened, but when putting others before yourself becomes a pattern in other areas of your life, there's a problem. There's a saying that describes codependency as "setting yourself on fire to keep someone else warm." That means codependent people will wear themselves out trying to "fix" someone else.

The following are all examples of codependency:

- Covering for someone's addiction, such as by calling their work and saying they're sick

- Staying home from an event because you are concerned your partner will get upset or relapse into addiction

- Going into debt to bail someone out of financial mistakes

- Asking someone for permission before making decisions

- Staying in a relationship with an abusive person

- Quitting a job because someone is relentless in telling you that you don't need to work

- Not taking care of yourself because you are attending to someone else's needs

- Taking care of someone when they have not requested it

- Trying to fix an issue for someone instead of just being supportive

The problem with codependency is that when you engage in these behaviors with someone who is abusive or gaslighting you, you become an *enabler*, meaning that you make excuses for or minimize the person's destructive behavior. You can also be an enabler if you witness abuse, especially of vulnerable people such as children or pets, and do not act to protect them. When you don't take action, it keeps you (and potentially others) caught in the cycle of abuse and reinforces your trauma bond with the abuser. If you think you may have codependent behaviors, please bring it up at your next therapy session.

Copyright © 2024 Sarkis Media LLC, *A Clinician's Guide to Gaslighting.* All rights reserved.

Are You Experiencing Codependency?

The following quiz will help you determine whether you are experiencing codependency with the gaslighter in your life. Place a check mark by each statement that applies to you.

☐   1.   I have called this person's work to make excuses for them not showing up.

☐   2.   I have missed work to take care of this person after they have exhibited unacceptable behavior.

☐   3.   I spend at least part of my day covering up for this person's behavior, particularly around my children.

☐   4.   When loved ones have spoken to me about this person's behavior, I joke about or downplay their concerns.

☐   5.   I have financially bailed this person out of legal trouble or paid their debts.

☐   6.   This person has shown no incentive to gain employment or contribute financially.

☐   7.   I have put off taking care of myself to help this person get their needs met.

☐   8.   It feels good to be needed to fix things for someone.

☐   9.   I get angry when someone doesn't appreciate the help I have given them (even if they didn't ask for help).

☐   10.   I stay in this relationship because I fear my partner will hurt or kill themselves.

If you marked one or more of these items, you might have codependent tendencies. Consider sharing these results with your therapist to discuss further.

Copyright © 2024 Sarkis Media LLC, *A Clinician's Guide to Gaslighting.* All rights reserved.

Guiding Clients Through No-Contact Versus Low-Contact

While it might seem that blocking someone's phone number, email, and social media accounts is a reasonably easy thing to do, it is an action that takes time and an extreme amount of emotional effort for your client. It's not the blocking itself that is so difficult; it's what it represents. Cutting off contact with a gaslighter means that your client has decided to move on from someone with whom they most likely have a trauma bond, giving up hope of reconciliation and being treated as well as they were during the idealization or love-bombing process.

Your client is also giving up hope of getting closure from the gaslighter. Not that gaslighters ever give any closure to their victims, but keeping communication open can make clients feel like there is a *chance* of it happening. Keeping contact open also offers clients the hope that how the gaslighter treated them is not the client's fault. However, they can also come to that conclusion during their work with you.

For some clients, going no-contact may not be an option, such as the case of a client who shares custody of children with a gaslighter. In that case, there are specific strategies your client can use to minimize contact while coparenting with the gaslighter (see chapter 11). Going no-contact may also not be an option when someone has business or legal obligations with the gaslighter. In these cases, a more feasible option is going low-contact, in which your client intentionally limits and reduces their contact and interactions with the gaslighter. Here are some examples of what going low-contact might look like:

- **Setting boundaries:** Your client must communicate and enforce boundaries with the gaslighter. For example, your client can specify their preferred methods and frequency of communication, such as restricting interactions to email or text messages and only responding to essential matters. They may also choose to restrict conversations to specific topics or refrain from engaging in discussions that trigger emotional distress or manipulation. Responding selectively and briefly to necessary communication can help maintain boundaries.

- **Limiting face-to-face interactions:** Your client minimizes any in-person encounters with the gaslighter and only meets in public or neutral settings where other people are present. This promotes safety and reduces the potential for manipulation or gaslighting tactics.

- **Seeking support networks:** It is important for your client to be surrounded by a robust support system of trusted friends, family, or group members who understand the dynamics of gaslighting and can provide validation and guidance. These individuals can offer emotional support and counteract the gaslighter's attempts to isolate and control the victim.

- **Utilizing technology:** To remain low-contact, your client can take advantage of technology to maintain distance and limit interactions. For example, if your client shares children with a gaslighter, they can limit communication to a coparenting app. They can also block the gaslighter's phone number, filter or redirect their emails, or use privacy settings on social media platforms to restrict the gaslighter's access to personal information.

Remember that every client's situation is unique, and the extent of contact will depend on their personal circumstances and safety considerations. Understand that going no-contact or low-contact is a heart-wrenching experience. Be aware of any attempts you are making to push your client toward an outcome you want. If your client is not yet willing to cut off contact with the gaslighter, know that going low-contact may be an intermediate step toward creating distance and eventually establishing no-contact if necessary for your client's safety and well-being. Be kind and remember that everyone works at their own pace.

**Client
Handout**

The Importance of Going No-Contact or Low-Contact with a Gaslighter

When dealing with a gaslighter, going no-contact or low-contact is one of the best ways to start healing and reclaiming your life. The more distance you put between yourself and a gaslighter, the more potential you have for healing. But what's the difference between no-contact and low-contact?

No-contact means that you refuse to engage in any communication with this person. This includes:

- Blocking their phone number, email, and social media accounts

- Not accepting messages from the person through third parties (known as "flying monkeys")

- Returning any letters or packages mailed to you by the person

However, there are times when going no-contact is not possible, such as when you have children with a gaslighter or when you must continue working with a gaslighter while you look for another job. In that case, you can consider going **low-contact** by:

- Asking to be transferred to another department or floor

- Asking to be taken off any team projects that include the person

- Inviting a supportive friend or family member to act as a "buffer" when you attend family gatherings

- Using a coparenting app instead of calling, texting, or emailing

- Using a neutral exchange point, a curbside exchange, or a trusted person as your proxy for transitions of custody

Copyright © 2024 Sarkis Media LLC, *A Clinician's Guide to Gaslighting*. All rights reserved.

The Trauma Bond with Aging Parents

Although an adult child is never obligated to care for an aging parent, especially one who has abused them through gaslighting and has not taken responsibility for their abusive behavior, there are nuances and cultural differences that often make it difficult for victims of gaslighting to go no-contact or low-contact with a family member. In particular, clients from collectivistic cultures may experience intense guilt and shame if they consider distancing themselves from an abusive parent. In a collectivist culture:

- Family members live at home until they are married.

- The family is considered when decisions are made.

- Loyalty to the family and community may be emphasized.

- Parents and grandparents must approve the client's college major, career, and marriage.

- There is a concept of "saving face" and not bringing shame to the family.

- The needs of the group are emphasized over the needs of the individual.

- Elders hold high esteem in the family and play a central role in decision-making.

In these cultures, there is often the assumption that adult children will care for aging parents and live in the same home with them—even if this parent has been a source of deep pain. If you are unfamiliar with a client's culture or the pressures they are experiencing, ask them. Never assume that you know what a client might be going through. Some clients may choose to provide caretaking for their parents but may organize other family members to share in these responsibilities to lessen the burden.

When a gaslighting parent dies, your client may feel various competing emotions at all once, including anger, relief, sadness, happiness, disappointment, regret, and pity. They may feel relief that they no longer have to deal with their parent's manipulation and abuse but also sadness for what they were subjected to. They may feel empathy or pity for the person their parent could have been. Emphasize that these feelings, although complicated and contradictory at times, are entirely understandable and normal for someone who has experienced the death of an emotionally unhealthy parent. To help your client work through their emotions, encourage them to focus on self-care— prioritizing what *they* need instead of what society or their family tells them they "should" be doing after a parent dies—and to treat themselves with self-compassion.

Your client may also need to set and maintain healthy boundaries even more than before. For example, they have the right not to attend any memorial or funeral service for their parent. Discuss the benefits and drawbacks of your client attending, and if attending will trigger trauma or otherwise hinder your client's well-being, give them "therapist permission" to not attend. They are not obligated to notify family members that they will not participate. Your client has a right to protect themselves and their well-being, even when those around them behave in a dysfunctional manner. Similarly, your client has the right not to have their deceased parent continue to assault their well-being through messages or recordings left for your client to be viewed after the parent's death. Your client has the right not to view anything left as a "surprise" by their parent.

Ultimately, you want your client to find ways to process their emotions about their parent's death and work to find their closure. Encourage them to use a journal for self-reflection or to create a memorial to say goodbye to their parent, both of which can be healing and cathartic. In addition, encourage them to lean on their friends, attend support groups, and continue therapy consistently. If you don't specialize in grief, consider supplementing your treatment with co-therapy with a clinician who specializes in complicated grief (see chapter 12).

CHAPTER 7

Trauma-Informed Treatment

Because gaslighting is a form of emotional abuse, it can trigger memories of past abuse that the client has experienced. This previous trauma may not necessarily involve emotional abuse but can include other forms, including physical, verbal, financial, sexual, or technological abuse. (See chapter 1 for more details about these forms of abuse.) Gaslighting can trigger trauma due to its manipulative and abusive nature, which undermines a person's sense of reality, erodes their self-esteem, and creates a power imbalance in the relationship. The gaslighter's tactics may also mirror the dynamics of previous abusive relationships, leading to a resurgence of trauma-related symptoms and distress. The victim may feel trapped, helpless, and powerless.

In this chapter, you will learn about complex posttraumatic stress disorder (C-PTSD) and the importance of engaging in trauma-informed care so you do not retraumatize clients. You will also discover how to teach clients about the nervous system's response to trauma and explore common trauma reactions, such as dissociation. To help clients progress in healing, you'll work with them to uncover the maladaptive coping strategies holding them back and identify healthy coping skills they can use instead. Finally, you will explore why victims of gaslighting are more likely to experience suicidality and discover assessment resources you can use to help clients stay safe.

C-PTSD and the Importance of Trauma-Informed Therapy

Complex posttraumatic stress disorder typically develops when a client has been persistently traumatized over a prolonged period—sometimes months or even years—though it can also occur after a client has experienced one particularly traumatic event. In either case, the person who experienced the trauma had little to no chance of escape at the time. Many experiences can lead to the development of C-PTSD, including child abuse, domestic violence, kidnapping, slavery, genocide, severe bullying, and long-term exposure to gaslighting and manipulation.

While C-PTSD is not recognized in the latest edition of the *Diagnostic and Statistical Manual of Mental Disorders* (DSM-5; APA, 2022), it is included in the *International Statistical Classification of Diseases and Related Health Problems* (ICD-11; WHO, 2022), which is the diagnostic manual used by a majority of medical professionals. According to the diagnostic criteria, C-PTSD differs from posttraumatic stress disorder (PTSD) in that it encompasses a broader range of symptoms that reflect the trauma's complex and enduring impact. In particular, when a person has C-PTSD, they meet criteria for PTSD plus one or more of the following (Brewin, 2020):

- Negative self-concept and persistent feelings of shame, self-doubt, and self-blame

- Intense and unpredictable emotional reactions, mood swings, difficulty managing emotions, and a sense of constant emotional distress

- Difficulty maintaining healthy relationships due to trust issues, fear of abandonment, difficulties with boundaries, isolation, and a heightened sense of vulnerability

Clients with C-PTSD struggle with feelings of worthlessness, shame, and guilt. Because they feel distrustful of others and the world, they have difficulty controlling their emotions and connecting with others. When these clients are subjected to gaslighting in their current relationships, they can experience retraumatization, leading to increased depression, anxiety, substance use, and suicidal ideation. If they experienced abuse or neglect as a child, they are also likely to have difficulties with attachment and lack positive social support, increasing their risk of suicidal ideation (Allbaugh et al., 2018).

Therefore, these clients will need a trauma-informed approach in therapy to prevent further traumatization. The aim of trauma-informed therapy is to help clients recover from trauma, focus on their strengths, and learn resiliency and coping strategies. The five guiding principles of trauma-informed psychotherapy are:

- **Safety:** Clients must feel a sense of safety and security in the therapeutic setting and process to disclose trauma.

- **Trustworthiness:** The therapist must first start building rapport for the client to gain a sense of trust.

- **Choice:** Clients must know that treatment is voluntary and that they have a choice in what to share in session.

- **Collaboration:** Therapy must be a collaboration between the therapist and the client. The therapist and client are not in the roles of "expert" and "novice." Both work together to help the client find hope, validation, and healing.

- **Empowerment:** The therapist must emphasize that the client is doing the work and not take credit for the client's growth.

Here are some ways to embody trauma-informed principles in practice:

- **Establish safety:** Create a safe and welcoming environment for your clients. Maintain a comfortable and private session space, ensure confidentiality, and set clear boundaries. If you provide telehealth sessions, use a HIPAA-compliant video service and see clients from a private room with no distractions. Ensure your body language and demeanor convey warmth, empathy, and nonjudgment. Avoid behaviors that might trigger feelings of unsafety or power imbalance, such as using authoritative language.

- **Build trust:** Be consistent, reliable, and transparent in your interactions. Practice active listening, validate your client's experiences, and show empathy and understanding. Avoid interrupting or dismissing their emotions or concerns. Allow your client to express themselves at their own pace, and validate their agency and autonomy in decision-making.

- **Empower choice:** Recognize and respect your client's autonomy and right to make choices. Offer options whenever possible and involve them in creating treatment plans and setting goals. Seek their input and collaborate on decisions that impact their treatment. Provide an informed consent document that explains your office policies and your client's rights in detail. When discussing interventions or strategies, explain their rationale and provide information to help the client make informed choices.

- **Recognize sensitivity to triggers:** Be aware of potential triggers and provide a safe space for clients to explore and process their trauma. Pay attention to their nonverbal cues, such as their body language, tone of voice, and signs of distress. If you notice signs of trauma, such as dissociation, respond compassionately and offer grounding techniques or self-regulation strategies to help them manage their emotions.

- **Maintain cultural sensitivity:** Be culturally sensitive and responsive in your counseling practice. Recognize and honor each client's diverse background, beliefs, and experiences. Avoid making assumptions or generalizations based on cultural stereotypes. Adapt your approach to meet the individual needs of each client, considering factors such as language, religion, customs, and social norms. Seek to understand your client's worldview and cultural norms.

Trauma-informed care is an ongoing learning, growth, and adaptation process. It requires continuous education, self-reflection, and a commitment to providing compassionate and empowering support to your clients. By embodying these principles, you can create a therapeutic space that promotes healing, growth, and resilience.

Trauma-Informed Interviewing

As a clinician, you may be part of a team that responds to 911 calls resulting from sexual assault or suicidal behavior. You may also be consulting with a team that interviews victims post-trauma. If so, you must be knowledgeable about trauma-informed interviewing protocol, which is a method for asking victims questions without triggering further trauma. This approach asks you to consider the following when supervising the questioning of a victim of abuse:

- Stay in the room the entire time a victim is being questioned.

- Ask the victim of abuse if they would prefer to speak in their primary language and have an interpreter present if English is their second language.

- Let the victim know they only need to answer questions if they feel comfortable doing so.

- Formulate questions in a way that doesn't assign guilt or responsibility. For example, "If you feel comfortable, could you tell me what happened last night?" "What do you remember hearing during the event?" "Are you able to tell me more about what happened last night?" "Can you tell me your thoughts and feelings during the event?"

- Focus on the three E's—event, experience, and effect:
    - The *events* or circumstances that caused the trauma
    - The client's *experience* of the event and any associated feelings (e.g., anger, helplessness)
    - The adverse physical, emotional, and psychological *effects* of the event (e.g., somatic symptoms, dissociation, nightmares)

- Avoid "why" questions when asking a victim about their abuse experience. For example, don't ask, "Why did you say that to him?" or "Why do you think this person targeted you?"

- Avoid asking for a chronology of events (e.g., do not ask, "And then what happened?")

Appropriate questions in trauma-informed interviewing include:

- Where would you like to start?

- Would you feel comfortable telling me what you can remember about your experience?

- When _____ (traumatic event) happened, what were your feelings and thoughts?

- What changed for you after _____ (traumatic event)?

Being Trauma-Informed

Use this worksheet to assess how you are currently applying the principles of trauma-informed care to your work with clients and how you could continue to improve.

1. **Safety:** These are the ways in which I make my clients feel physically and emotionally welcome in my practice:

   _____

   _____

   _____

   These are areas in which I could improve:

   _____

   _____

   _____

2. **Trustworthiness:** These are the ways that I remain a stable and supportive presence for my clients:

   _____

   _____

   _____

   These are areas in which I could improve:

   _____

   _____

   _____

3. **Choice:** These are the ways I show my clients that they have control over their treatment:

   _____

   _____

   _____

These are areas in which I could improve:

_____

_____

_____

4. **Collaboration:** These are the ways I work with clients on mutually established goals:

_____

_____

_____

These are areas in which I could improve:

_____

_____

_____

5. **Empowerment:** These are the ways I recognize my client's strengths and resilience:

_____

_____

_____

These are areas in which I could improve:

_____

_____

_____

 Copyright © 2024 Sarkis Media LLC, *A Clinician's Guide to Gaslighting*. All rights reserved.

Trauma Responses

Gaslighting can trigger a trauma response because it activates the same neural pathways associated with the sympathetic nervous system's fight, flight, freeze, and fawn responses. These are profoundly ingrained survival mechanisms that help individuals respond to perceived threats or danger. When a client is exposed to gaslighting behaviors, one of these survival responses is likely to reemerge:

- **Fight:** The client feels a strong urge to defend themselves, their reality, and their sense of self. They may become argumentative, aggressive, or defensive to counter the gaslighter's tactics and reclaim their truth.

- **Flight:** The client feels an intense urge to escape or avoid the gaslighting situation, leading them to withdraw, become emotionally distant, or seek physical distance from the gaslighter to self-preserve.

- **Freeze:** The client feels paralyzed and unable to respond effectively to the gaslighter's manipulation. They may experience a sense of powerlessness, confusion, or cognitive dissonance as the gaslighter's tactics undermine their perception of reality. This response can stem from past trauma where freezing was a survival strategy to avoid further harm.

- **Fawn:** The client feels compelled to please or appease the gaslighter to mitigate the abuse or maintain a semblance of safety. They may become compliant, submissive, or excessively accommodating, attempting to meet the gaslighter's demands and avoid conflict.

Of these survival responses, the fawn response is perhaps one of the most common, as many clients trapped in the cycle of gaslighting will resort to this response if there is a strong trauma bond between them and their abuser. By appeasing their abuser and disconnecting from their own needs, they avoid further confrontation. Unfortunately, this only furthers the dysfunctional pattern of codependency and opens the client up to further victimization over the long term. The fawn response can also be a source of guilt and shame for clients, who may feel like they should have "fought back" against the other person.

One way to help clients combat this self-judgment is to externalize the brain when discussing your client's sympathetic nervous system response to trauma. Explain to your client that when someone is confronted with a situation that is deemed threatening, such as emotional abuse, the human brain will automatically react in a way that most likely leads to survival. Sometimes this involves fighting back against the threat (fight), running away from it (flight), going numb or immobile (freeze), or reverting to people-pleasing behaviors (fawn). This process, which happens in milliseconds, is one over which we have little conscious control. Let your client know that the human brain doesn't let people "pick" their reactions—the brain does it automatically. Externalizing the brain in such a manner helps reduce your client's guilt and shame.

**Therapist
Handout**

Externalizing the Brain

The "empty chair" technique is a powerful therapeutic tool that can help clients externalize their thoughts, their feelings, or other parts of themselves. By treating an aspect of the self as outside of the self, clients can engage in a dialogue with these parts of themselves, allowing them to gain insight, understanding, and resolution. This exercise focuses on externalizing the brain, enabling the client to separate themselves from distressing thoughts and gain a new perspective. Because this technique may bring up intense emotions or thoughts for your client, proceed gently. If at any point your client feels overwhelmed, take a break and process their experience.

Preparation

- Ensure that the therapy space is quiet, comfortable, and free of distractions.

- Place an empty chair in front of the client.

Setting the Intention

- Take a few moments to do a centering exercise with your client, such as practicing deep breathing, doing a mental scan of the body, or inviting the client to focus on their senses. Remind your client that they are in a safe and supportive space to explore and understand their thoughts and feelings.

Externalizing the Brain

- Ask your client to imagine that their brain is a separate entity—an external character—sitting in the empty chair. Encourage them to visualize it as vividly as possible, giving it a distinct appearance, such as a person or an animated figure.

Opening the Dialogue

- Invite your client to speak out loud to their externalized brain in the empty chair. Have your client address it directly, acknowledging its presence in the chair.

- Encourage your client to express their thoughts and feelings, letting the externalized brain know how it affects them.

- Ask your client share any specific concerns, worries, or patterns of thinking they would like to explore. For example, your client may be angry with their brain for freezing during a traumatic situation or for making them feel like they weren't good enough.

 Copyright © 2024 Sarkis Media LLC, *A Clinician's Guide to Gaslighting*. All rights reserved.

Role Reversal

- Now, invite your client to switch chairs and take on the role of the externalized brain. Ask them to imagine themselves as the externalized brain, responding to their previous statements in the other chair.

- Have your client speak from the perspective of the externalized brain, providing insights, explanations, or even challenges to their concerns and thoughts.

Engage in Dialogue

- Continue facilitating the dialogue between your client and their externalized brain, inviting them to switch roles and chairs as needed.

- Encourage them to ask questions, seek clarification, and express any emotions or concerns that arise during the conversation.

- Give your client permission to speak honestly and openly, allowing for a genuine exploration of their internal dynamics.

Reflection and Integration

- Once you feel the dialogue has reached a natural conclusion, take a moment with your client to reflect on the insights gained and the emotions they experienced during the exercise.

- Consider any new perspectives or resolutions from the dialogue and share them with your client if appropriate.

Closing

- End the exercise by inviting the client to express gratitude to themselves and to the externalized brain for engaging in this process.

- Guide your client in taking a few deep breaths, grounding themselves in the present moment and allowing the insights to settle.

Copyright © 2024 Sarkis Media LLC, *A Clinician's Guide to Gaslighting*. All rights reserved.

Dissociative Episodes

Dissociative episodes are prevalent among trauma victims and can emerge when your clients are experiencing gaslighting and other forms of abuse. Dissociation is a complex psychological phenomenon that serves as a survival tactic during immense stress, trauma, or overwhelming emotions. It involves a disconnection or detachment from one's thoughts, feelings, sensations, or memories, creating a sense of distance or numbness from the present moment. Dissociation can manifest along a continuum, ranging from mild experiences of "spacing out" or daydreaming to more severe forms such as dissociative amnesia or identity disturbance.

Dissociation serves several adaptive functions that aid in survival during traumatic experiences:

- **Reduction of emotional and sensory overload:** Dissociation helps to compartmentalize distressing emotions and overwhelming sensory information, providing temporary relief from the intensity of the traumatic experience. Creating psychological distance from the experience can prevent it from feeling too overwhelming to process.

- **Preservation of a coherent sense of self:** Dissociation can help clients maintain a cohesive sense of self by separating the traumatic experiences or memories from their core identity. This separation allows people to continue functioning and adapting to their environment without being constantly consumed by the trauma.

- **Regulation of the stress response:** Dissociation can help regulate the body's stress response system by dampening the physiological and emotional arousal associated with trauma. By disconnecting from the overwhelming stressors, dissociation aids in managing the autonomic nervous system's heightened state of activation, promoting a sense of safety and self-preservation.

While dissociation can be adaptive and necessary during the acute phase of trauma, prolonged or chronic dissociation can impede your client's ability to process and integrate traumatic experiences. For example, they may dissociate during session when discussing an aspect of their past trauma history that has not been revealed previously in therapy. Remembering an event that was once "locked away" can be startling and can raise feelings of fear. The following are warning signs that your client may be dissociating:

- They don't remember portions of your conversation earlier in the same session.
- They "drift off" when discussing something trauma-related.
- They avoid making eye contact with you due to being detached from reality.
- They appear to lose balance or possibly faint.
- They physically freeze.

It is essential to approach dissociation with sensitivity and provide therapeutic interventions that promote safety, stabilization, and gradual reconnection with the self and the traumatic experiences. When your client dissociates during a session, gently acknowledge to your client what you have witnessed and describe dissociation as a normal response when someone is triggered by trauma.

You can then walk your client through a grounding or centering technique to help them manage overwhelming emotions, reconnect with the present moment, and regain a sense of stability and control. Here is an example of a grounding exercise you can try:

1. Begin by inviting your client to find a comfortable seated position, with their feet flat on the floor and their hands resting on their lap.

2. Ask them to take a few deep breaths, inhaling slowly through their nose and exhaling through their mouth, allowing their body to relax with each breath.

3. Have them direct their attention to their physical sensations, encouraging them to notice the feeling of their feet on the ground, the weight of their body in the chair, and the sensation of their breath moving in and out.

4. Next, guide them to focus on their senses. Ask them to name three things they can see in their immediate environment, three things they can feel (such as the texture of their clothes or the temperature of the air), and three things they can hear.

5. Encourage your client to continue taking slow, deep breaths as they engage with their senses. Remind them to observe each sensation without judgment or attachment, simply allowing themselves to be present in the moment.

6. If your client notices their mind starting to wander or intrusive thoughts arising, gently guide them back to their grounding points—the physical sensations, their senses, and their breath.

7. Conclude the exercise by asking your client to acknowledge any shifts in their state of mind or body, and remind them that they can return to this grounding practice whenever they need to reconnect with the present moment.

Incorporating grounding and centering techniques into therapy sessions can help your clients learn to combat dissociation or depersonalization outside of session as well. You'll also want to ask your client how often they experience dissociation and which sensory information triggers it, such as certain sights, sounds, or smells. Ask your client to keep track of their dissociative episodes, including their potential triggers. Once they become more aware of their dissociative episodes, they may notice that these episodes naturally decrease in frequency and intensity.

Grounding and Centering Techniques

When someone is triggered by trauma, it is a common and normal response for them to dissociate—to feel disconnected from their thoughts, feelings, sensations, or memories. Dissociation creates a sense of distance or numbness from the present moment so that the trauma does not feel so overwhelming. However, dissociating can also prevent you from healing if you continue to dissociate when you are in a safe environment and are trying to process a past trauma (such as when you are in therapy) or when you are triggered by something that does not pose a threat but reminds you of a past trauma (such as meeting a new coworker whose voice sounds similar to someone who abused you).

When this happens, grounding and centering techniques can help you reconnect with your body and the present moment. Try out the following techniques and see which ones you would like to practice when you notice you are dissociating. Continue or repeat the exercise you have chosen until you have returned to baseline. "Baseline" can be different for everyone, but it involves feeling calmer, more like yourself, and more attuned or focused. It may not be exactly how you want to feel, but it's good enough to complete necessary tasks and stay present when someone is talking with you.

Deep Breathing

Inhale for a count of 5 and then exhale for a count of 10. (You can adjust these counts if needed—please do not overstrain yourself. The important part is to make the exhale at least a couple seconds longer than the inhale.) Repeat three times and then check in with yourself to see if you are feeling less anxiety. You can continue this process until you feel a sense of calm.

Name Three Things

Name three things you can feel, three things you can hear, and three things you can see. If you are not yet at baseline, continue naming more things you can feel, hear, and see until you notice you are more attuned to your senses and the present moment.

Go for a Walk

Get outside and take a walk, whether it is for 15 minutes or an hour. Being outdoors can help you refocus, especially if you were in a triggering environment. Focus on your senses, such as how the breeze feels on your face, the warmth of the sun, and the weight of your feet connecting with the ground as you walk.

Copyright © 2024 Sarkis Media LLC, *A Clinician's Guide to Gaslighting*. All rights reserved.

Client Worksheet

Tracking When You Dissociate

Dissociation is how your brain "checks out" when you are under stress or triggered by reminders of a past traumatic event. When people dissociate, some feel like they are floating above themselves, while others get hazy vision. Other symptoms can include losing track of time, feeling emotionally numb, having gaps in your memory, and feeling like the world around you isn't real. Use this log to track the dates and times of your dissociative episodes, the preceding event before each episode, any emotions or body sensations you felt, how long the episode lasted, what stopped it, and the possible triggers that caused it.

Date/Time	Preceding Event	Emotions	Body Sensations	Duration	What Stopped It	Triggers

Coping Mechanisms

Trauma victims in gaslighting relationships often resort to maladaptive or unhealthy coping strategies to survive the abusive dynamics. They may deny or suppress their emotions, convince themselves that the abuse isn't happening or minimize its impact, isolate themselves from loved ones, or use drugs or alcohol to numb their emotional pain. Moving toward healthy coping strategies is essential for survivors of gaslighting to regain their emotional well-being and rebuild their lives. This can include reestablishing their support network, prioritizing self-care (see chapter 10), developing assertiveness skills, and learning how to set healthy boundaries.

As a mental health professional, you can guide clients toward healthier coping strategies by providing psychoeducation about the impact of gaslighting, helping them understand the dynamics of abuse, validating their experiences, and offering tools and techniques to navigate their healing journey. It is important that you collaboratively set goals, develop personalized coping strategies for your client, and provide ongoing support and encouragement to facilitate the client's movement toward healing and resolution.

Unhealthy Coping Mechanisms

When people have experienced trauma, they tend to use coping mechanisms that make things feel "right" again, even if these coping mechanisms come at a high cost or ultimately make things worse, like drinking alcohol excessively. Use this checklist to identify any unhealthy strategies you have used to cope in the past or still use today.

❒ Sleeping too much

❒ Using drugs or alcohol

❒ Impulsively spending

❒ Overeating or undereating

❒ Procrastinating or avoiding important tasks

❒ Isolating from others

❒ Comparing yourself to others

❒ Overreacting to small issues

❒ Worrying excessively

❒ Romanticizing the past

❒ Avoiding anything that isn't "positive"

❒ Overusing social media

❒ Engaging in unsafe sexual activity

❒ Self-mutilating (such as cutting or burning)

❒ Running away

Copyright © 2024 Sarkis Media LLC, *A Clinician's Guide to Gaslighting*. All rights reserved.

Healthy Coping Skills:
A Psychological "First Aid" Kit

Healthy coping strategies can help you process your trauma and endure difficult moments. To begin, think of a scale from 1 to 10, where 1 is the worst you've felt, and 10 is the best you've felt. What number are you at on that scale right now? What's one thing you could do to raise yourself to the next number on the scale?

Put a check mark by any healthy coping strategies you feel connected to or might enjoy that would enhance your score on this scale. Keep this list where it is easily accessible, or take a photo and save it in a "favorites" album on your phone. When you're stressed, check in with yourself and use the strategies you've identified here.

- ❑ Take a bath
- ❑ Go for a walk or hike
- ❑ Talk to a friend
- ❑ Watch a movie
- ❑ Read a book
- ❑ Draw or paint
- ❑ Meditate or pray
- ❑ Dance
- ❑ Play with your kids
- ❑ Snuggle your pet
- ❑ Listen to music
- ❑ Declutter your space
- ❑ Learn something new

- ❑ Do something for another person
- ❑ Hug yourself or someone else
- ❑ Put together a puzzle
- ❑ Garden
- ❑ Exercise
- ❑ Plan a fun adventure
- ❑ Cook
- ❑ Play a musical instrument
- ❑ Invite a friend to lunch
- ❑ Take a day off from work
- ❑ Take a nap
- ❑ Do a visualization or progressive muscle relaxation exercise

Copyright © 2024 Sarkis Media LLC, *A Clinician's Guide to Gaslighting*. All rights reserved.

Suicidality and Safety Planning

Due to the destructive nature of emotional abuse, clients in gaslighting relationships are at increased risk of suicidality, especially once they have gone no-contact or low-contact with their abuser. Withdrawal from the trauma bond can also lead to suicidal behavior because the victim may feel deeply attached to and reliant on the abuser. When the bond is threatened or severed, it can lead to overwhelming feelings of emptiness, loss, and despair, all of which can contribute to thoughts of suicide. The following are some additional factors that can increase the risk of suicidality among victims of gaslighting:

- **Manipulation and control:** Trauma bonds involve a power dynamic where the abuser may use tactics such as gaslighting, emotional blackmail, or threats to maintain dominance over the victim. This manipulation can lead to feelings of helplessness, worthlessness, and a distorted sense of reality, further exacerbating suicidal ideation. The likelihood of suicide increases proportionately to the length of time your client has been exposed to gaslighting and other abusive behaviors.

- **Isolation and dependency:** Abusive relationships often isolate the victim from their external support systems, which can contribute to a sense of hopelessness and intensify suicidal thoughts, as the victim may perceive no way out of the distressing circumstances.

- **Trauma reenactment and self-blame:** Since trauma bonds can be rooted in past traumatic experiences, the victim may subconsciously reenact these patterns in their current relationship, perpetuating a cycle of trauma in which the victim believes they are unworthy of love or deserving of the mistreatment, further fueling suicidal thoughts and feelings of guilt or shame.

- **Complex emotions and conflicting loyalties:** Trauma bonds often involve love, fear, and loyalty toward the abuser. The victim may experience conflicting emotions—torn between their need for love and validation and their awareness of the harmful nature of the relationship—which create intense psychological distress and increase the risk of suicidality as the victim grapples with the complex dynamics of the trauma bond.

Risk Factors for Suicidality in Victims of Gaslighting

- Continued contact with the gaslighter
- History of abuse in their family of origin
- Family history of suicide
- Treatment-resistant depression
- Low self-concept
- Impulsive personality
- Substance abuse
- Insecure attachment style (Boroujerdi et al., 2019)

If your client is having thoughts of harming themselves or you believe they are at risk, it is essential to conduct a thorough suicide risk assessment to determine the severity of the client's suicidal ideation, any previous suicide attempts, and the presence of protective factors. The more detailed the examination, the more likely you will accurately identify suicidal behavior. Consider using one of the following scales:

- **Ask Suicide-Screening Questions Toolkit** (ASQ; Horowitz et al., 2012, 2020): A clinician-completed scale consisting of five yes/no questions.

- **Columbia Suicide Severity Rating Scale** (C-SSRS; Posner et al., 2011): A clinician-completed standardized scale consisting of six yes/no questions.

- **Patient Health Questionnaire** (PHQ-9; Kroenke & Spitzer, 2002): A client-completed scale consisting of ten yes/no questions, created for screening and measuring a client's severity of depression.

After assessing the client's level of risk, it is crucial to develop an evidence-based safety plan if the client is experiencing suicidal thoughts. When working with a client who is suicidal, it is essential to follow specific guidelines and take appropriate actions. Here are some steps you can take:

- **Establish a crisis response protocol:** Collaborate with your client to create a crisis response protocol that outlines specific steps they will take in a suicide crisis. This may involve identifying emergency contacts, crisis hotlines, or nearby mental health facilities. This chapter includes a safety plan that your client can complete with your guidance.

- **Identify coping strategies:** Work with your client to identify healthy coping strategies they can utilize during distress. This may include engaging in self-care activities, reaching out to loved ones, or using grounding techniques.

- **List the client's support network:** Identify trusted people in your client's life who can provide support during difficult times. These may include family members, friends, or other professionals involved in their care.

- **Restrict access to lethal means:** Assess and address potential access to lethal means, such as firearms, medications, or other objects that could be used for self-harm. Collaborate with the client to develop strategies for limiting access to these means. Options include having trusted friends and family members remove lethal items from your client's home.

- **Develop an immediate crisis response plan:** Outline specific steps your client can take in an acute crisis, including when and how to seek immediate help, such as contacting emergency services or going to the nearest emergency room.

- **Regularly review and update the safety plan:** Safety plans should be regularly reviewed and updated with clients to ensure their effectiveness. Encourage open communication with your client about any changes in their thoughts, feelings, relationships, or circumstances that may require adjustments to the plan.

Even with the best assessment and clinical skills, you may still have a client who dies by suicide. It's a devastating fact of being a clinician. There is only so much you can do. You can do everything right and be the most seasoned clinician, yet your client may still end their life. The thought that you could have done something differently can haunt you and lead to burnout. When this happens, it is vital to seek supervision or therapy to help you process the experience and grieve appropriately. And if at any time you find that a client's suicide is causing you to experience thoughts of harming yourself, please get in touch with 988 or 988lifeline.org.

Safety Plan

A safety plan can help you when you are in crisis or suicidal. Fill out this worksheet and review it step by step until you feel safe. Keep this plan in a location where it is easily accessible. You can also take a photo of it with your phone and save it in a "favorites" album. Review this worksheet with your clinician at least once per year to make needed updates.

1. **Triggers and warning signs:** What are your triggers? What are some warning signs (e.g., changes in thoughts, mood, behavior) that let you know you have been triggered?

   _____

   _____

   _____

   _____

2. **Coping strategies:** What can you do to distract yourself or feel better? What has worked for you in the past? What would you encourage a friend or loved one to do if they were in the same situation?

   _____

   _____

   _____

   _____

3. **People and places to distract yourself:** Whom can you contact to distract yourself? What places can you go to (e.g., restaurant, movie theater) to distract yourself?

   Name: _____ Phone: _____

   Name: _____ Phone: _____

   Places: _____

   _____

   _____

   _____

Copyright © 2024 Sarkis Media LLC, *A Clinician's Guide to Gaslighting.* All rights reserved.

4. **People and organizations to support you:** Which trusted individuals, professionals, and services can you contact when you're in crisis?

Therapist name: _____ Phone: _____

Local hospital: _____ Phone: _____

Other: _____ Phone: _____

988 Suicide & Crisis Lifeline: Call or text 988

5. **Safe environment:** What can you do to make your home or surroundings safer (e.g., removing lethal items from your home)?

_____

_____

_____

_____

_____

_____

Copyright © 2024 Sarkis Media LLC, *A Clinician's Guide to Gaslighting.* All rights reserved.

Remembering a Client Who Died by Suicide

Having a client die by suicide can profoundly impact you. One technique that can help you process your feelings is to write an unsent letter to your client. In this letter, you might want to include an acknowledgment of your loss; remembrances of your client and the progress they made in treatment; an acknowledgment of your client's struggles; gratitude for the time you had together and the chance to get to know your client; any feelings of inadequacy, hopelessness, or anger you've felt as a clinician; any feelings of forgiveness or understanding toward your client; and any hopes or wishes you have for your client, such as the hope that they have found relief from their pain. When you're done, please consider sharing your letter with your therapist.

_____

_____

_____

_____

_____

_____

_____

_____

_____

_____

_____

_____

_____

_____

_____

_____

_____

_____

Copyright © 2024 Sarkis Media LLC, *A Clinician's Guide to Gaslighting.* All rights reserved.

CHAPTER 8

Boundaries

As clinicians, our primary goal is to provide compassionate and effective care to our clients, help them navigate their unique challenges, and facilitate their journey toward healing and growth. Central to this process when working with victims of gaslighting is teaching them how to rediscover, establish, and maintain appropriate boundaries. Although they may have been able to set healthy limits in the past, the nature of gaslighting is that it systematically dismantles a person's ability to advocate for themselves and enforce their boundaries. As a result, clients trapped in gaslighting relationships often have poor boundaries characterized by overly accommodating behavior, difficulty saying no, an inability to self-advocate, tolerance of mistreatment, and emotional dependency. They fear conflict and prioritize "keeping the peace" over addressing issues or standing up for themselves, leading to a pattern of accepting mistreatment.

In this chapter, you'll discover how to help your client learn about porous versus rigid boundaries and review the steps needed to enforce healthy boundaries with a gaslighter. Part of this work will involve supporting your client as they rediscover their values and remember what is important to them. You will also explore an effective technique your client can use when interacting with a gaslighter: the gray rock method. Finally, you will teach your client how to handle boundary violations they may encounter from flying monkeys or people sent to hoover your client back into a gaslighting relationship.

Boundary Problems

Salvador Minuchin (1974), the founder of structural family therapy, explained that there are three types of boundaries: diffuse (enmeshed), rigid (disengaged), and clear (healthy). Most people have a mix of boundary types, and victims of gaslighting often have both diffuse and rigid boundaries.

Diffuse boundaries are found in families with little independence among family members. People's feelings depend on how others in the family system feel. Clients with this boundary type have difficulty making decisions without seeking validation or approval, and they rely heavily on others for emotional support and guidance. They also exhibit an anxious attachment style and fear rejection if they don't meet others' demands. They have difficulty saying no to requests and allow people to take advantage of their time, resources, or personal space. They can become overly involved in other people's issues and try to "fix" them instead of offering support. A person with diffuse boundaries may overshare with others as well. In therapy, these clients may become excessively dependent on their therapist, have difficulty containing their emotions during sessions, and frequently express intense feelings or have emotional outbursts that go beyond the immediate context of therapy.

Rigid boundaries are found in families with limited communication and emotional expression. Clients with rigid boundaries often have an avoidant attachment style, leading them to avoid intimacy and close relationships. They may seem detached and keep themselves far from others to avoid rejection. They tend to be very private and may not disclose personal information to others. In therapy, these clients tend to keep their emotions guarded and may find it challenging to express or connect with their feelings. They might resist exploring vulnerable or sensitive topics—maintaining a stoic or distant demeanor—and reveal limited information about themselves. They may take offense when you ask questions about their feelings or experiences, resist feedback or suggestions, and dismiss therapeutic interventions as unnecessary or irrelevant. This can make it difficult to achieve progress in sessions.

Finally, *clear boundaries* are found in families who feel comfortable experiencing their feelings and addressing concerns without fear of retaliation. People with clear boundaries know their wants and needs and will say no when a request doesn't fit their schedule or values. They appropriately share information and do not tend to overshare or undershare. Clear boundaries are most often seen in people with a secure attachment style. As a clinician, your role when working with victims of gaslighting is to help them create new, clear boundaries or reestablish any clear boundaries that were eroded by the gaslighter.

What Type of Boundaries Do You Have?

In relationships, *boundaries* are the limits you set with other people to protect your physical, emotional, and psychological well-being. Boundaries help define the space between yourself and others, determining what you find acceptable and unacceptable when it comes to behavior, communication, and personal space. There are three types of boundaries: diffuse, rigid, and clear.

When you have **diffuse boundaries**, you don't draw much of a line between yourself and others. You may automatically say yes to everyone (when you are asked to participate in social activities, take on extra roles at work, etc.) but then feel overburdened and resentful as a result. Similarly, if someone invades your personal space, you might allow yourself to feel uncomfortable instead of telling the person they need to back up. Overall, you have difficulty being assertive when you need help or want to talk about a concern because you fear this will lead to rejection. You may also have a tendency to overshare with others, or to get overinvolved in your friends' and family members' issues by trying to "fix" them, and regret it later. You may have developed this boundary type if you were in a gaslighting relationship where the other person told you that you didn't have a right to set boundaries.

If someone has gaslit you, you may have developed **rigid boundaries**, putting up a wall around you to protect yourself. You avoid experiencing feelings and tend to talk yourself out of feeling intense emotions. You may be wary of sharing any personal information with others and find comfort in being in control at home or in social situations. You avoid being vulnerable, even with those closest to you, because you believe that vulnerability shows weakness. As a result, you may find it too risky to be in a committed relationship because you are afraid you will get hurt and lose your independence. You may also be self-critical when you make mistakes.

When you have **clear boundaries**, you make decisions that match your values and beliefs. You don't accept guilt or shame from others and you expect others to treat you with courtesy and respect. When you need help, you can reach out to someone and still feel good about yourself. You can quickly identify when someone is gaslighting or manipulating you, and you take steps to create a healthy distance from that person. If a friend or family member sets a clear boundary with you, you respect it, and it doesn't change how you feel about that person. If someone says you've hurt them, you apologize and accept accountability instead of becoming defensive.

Most people have a mix of boundary types, and boundaries can vary across different relationships and situations as well. For example, you may have diffuse boundaries with a gaslighting family member and clear boundaries with a supportive friend. If someone in your life is a gaslighter, you may find yourself being guilted and shamed into having diffuse boundaries. One of the goals of therapy is to help you develop clear boundaries across various interactions and situations.

Copyright © 2024 Sarkis Media LLC, *A Clinician's Guide to Gaslighting*. All rights reserved.

The Gray Rock Method

As much as your clients try to go no-contact or low-contact with a gaslighter, they may still have to interact with them at least occasionally. One way your clients can successfully handle interactions with a gaslighter is by using the *gray rock method*. With this method, your client responds as if they were a gray rock—unemotive, unresponsive, bland, and even dull. They refrain from giving the gaslighter any information or details about their life, stick to facts only, give brief answers, and spend only a limited amount of time with the gaslighter. Because gaslighters feed off another person's emotions, having your client react with little to no emotion can thwart the gaslighter's attempt to manipulate your client.

Some clients may feel concerned that they are being rude or not acting in a way that is congruent with their true selves when they use the gray rock method. You can turn these feelings into therapeutic moments by discussing any concerns the client has about potentially upsetting other people. Remind your client that they do not have control over others' feelings. By refusing to respond to the gaslighter's attempts to criticize or cause drama, they are simply enacting a healthy boundary.

It is important to let your client know that there can be side effects to using the gray rock method with a gaslighter. In particular, gaslighters may initially escalate their behaviors when they see they are not getting a response from an intended victim. The gaslighter may see the gray rock method as a challenge and try to get closer to the victim to see how long it takes them to break down. However, if the gaslighter is consistently met with indifference and bland answers, they will usually move on to another victim. Encourage your client to remain steadfast with this method for it to be most effective.

The Gray Rock Technique

Gaslighters feed off any emotions you give them. For that reason, when a gaslighter triggers you or tries to manipulate you, you want to provide them with a response that is as boring, disinterested, and neutral as possible. This form of communication is known as the "gray rock" method because your goal is to respond like a gray rock would: by being dull and unresponsive. This includes keeping any interactions with the gaslighter as brief as possible, limiting what you share about yourself, and focusing on factual details rather than your or the gaslighter's feelings. Remember, you are not responsible for their feelings; you are simply enacting a healthy boundary.

A key component of the gray rock method is giving only brief, emotionless replies to the gaslighter's attempts to provoke you. For example, if they tell you, "I never said that. You're crazy," consider responding with any of the following statements:

- "That's interesting."

- "Oh, okay."

- "Sure."

- "Okay, if you say so."

- "Maybe."

- "Uh-huh."

- "Hm."

- "I see."

You want to speak in a neutral tone and act as disinterested as possible. These responses don't confirm that the gaslighter is correct, but they don't indicate that they are wrong either. Gaslighters work in absolutes, so it throws them off when you give them an ambiguous answer. They can't get high off your emotions, making them less likely to try to pull you into their drama.

However, there are some drawbacks to the gray rock method. At first, the gaslighter may try even harder to wear you down—so you should be prepared to hold fast and consistently practice this method until they realize that their efforts are futile. In addition, the gray rock method works best as a short-term solution. The most effective way to deal with a gaslighter is to go no-contact or low-contact.

Copyright © 2024 Sarkis Media LLC, *A Clinician's Guide to Gaslighting*. All rights reserved.

Helping Your Client Set Healthy Boundaries

Step 1: Discover Your Client's Values

Because our boundaries are informed by what we value in life, the first step in helping your client set healthy boundaries with gaslighters is to work with them to uncover their values, purpose, and priorities. This journey of self-discovery can be difficult for many clients, as they have been caught in a relationship with someone who has ridiculed their beliefs, continually violated their limits, and gone into a rage whenever the victim attempted to set a boundary. For those reasons, your client may be unsure of what they value.

To help your client rediscover their values, ask them to identify times in their life when they felt the most fulfilled, alive, and content. These memories can act like the client's North Star, guiding them to what is most important to them. They can also reflect on how they might want people to describe them decades from now, reflecting on what they hope to have accomplished. They might even share what life lessons they wish to impart to their children or nieces and nephews. Once your client has identified their core values in life, they can better identify when those values are being violated, which leads to the next step in setting a boundary.

Step 2: Identify the Boundary Violation

At this stage, your client identifies the behavior the gaslighter has engaged in that violates their values. For example, if the client values respect and kindness, their boundaries may be violated if the gaslighter yells at them. If the client values honesty and transparency, their boundaries may be violated whenever the gaslighter lies or omits essential information. Or if the client values calmness and emotional sobriety, they may experience a boundary violation when the gaslighter loudly accuses them of bad behavior in front of family and friends.

Step 3: State the Need or Limit

Finally, the client must state what they need or what behaviors from the gaslighter they will no longer tolerate—and, importantly, what actions they will take in response to such boundary violations. For example, if your client is on the phone with a gaslighter who starts yelling, your client can respond with a simple "If you continue to yell, I will end the call." The hardest step for your client may be following through and ending the call.

If the gaslighter tries to convince them of something that never happened, your client can respond with "I know what I saw was real." Or if a gaslighter tries to embarrass your client in front of family and friends, the client can respond with "That's inappropriate" or "That's not true" and then walk away.

Since gaslighters will inevitably continue to disrespect and push back on boundaries, it is essential to prepare clients for this possibility. When this occurs, remind your client that how the gaslighter responds to the boundary is not the client's responsibility. If the gaslighter responds inappropriately, it doesn't mean your client shouldn't have set a boundary. Instead, encourage your client to use the gray rock method described earlier, which can stop the gaslighter from getting a payoff. Sometimes, your client may also choose to walk away without stating a boundary. Setting a boundary doesn't necessarily need to be done with words—walking away can be more powerful. Usually, the best option with a gaslighter is to go no-contact or low-contact.

For many clients, boundary work is daunting. To remind them of their strengths, you can use a solution-focused therapy technique, asking the client about previous times they successfully advocated for themselves or for others, such as their children or friends. Reinforcing the times in your client's life when they demonstrated good boundaries can help them find the motivation to do so again. Let your client know that enforcing boundaries is a difficult and courageous thing to do.

What Are Your Values?

Values are the guiding principles by which we run our lives. Values may be acquired from or taught by your family, culture, religion, organizations, and society. Circle which values you identify with most. You can also add your own values to the list.

Acceptance	Generosity	Mindfulness
Balance	Gratitude	Neatness
Bravery	Growth	Openness
Calmness	Harmony	Optimism
Commitment	Health	Peace
Communication	Helpfulness	Persistence
Community	Honesty	Reliability
Compassion	Honor	Respect
Confidence	Hope	Security
Consistency	Humility	Self-love
Conviction	Humor	Sensitivity
Courage	Independence	Service
Courtesy	Inspiration	Sincerity
Creativity	Integrity	Sobriety
Decisiveness	Intuition	Togetherness
Discernment	Joy	Transparency
Empathy	Justice	Trust
Encouragement	Kindness	Truth
Endurance	Knowledge	Wisdom
Energy	Leadership	Wonder
Expressiveness	Learning	Working hard
Fairness	Love	
Faith	Loyalty	
Freedom	Manners	

Copyright © 2024 Sarkis Media LLC, *A Clinician's Guide to Gaslighting*. All rights reserved.

Enforcing Your Boundaries

It can be challenging to enforce boundaries when someone in your life seems to make it their sole purpose to violate the limits you set with them. When you start setting boundaries, it can feel very uncomfortable and even scary. You are potentially changing the dynamic of your relationship. To make this process easier, follow these steps when setting a boundary:

1. **State the boundary violation:** Explain what the other person did to disrespect your values. Use clear, straightforward language.

2. **State your need or limit:** Let the other person know what you need or are unwilling to tolerate. If the other person is making a request of you, you can say no.

For example:

- If your partner is looking through your phone and accusing you of cheating:

  "Looking through my phone is a violation of my privacy. It's not okay with me, and I need you to stop right now. I won't be in a relationship with someone who doesn't respect me or my belongings."

- If your mother tells your children they don't need to listen to you:

  "Telling my children they don't need to listen to me undermines my parenting. My children already have a parent. If you continue, I will need to stop contact."

- If your boss tells you they must meet with you but they refuse to have a witness in the room:

  "Not allowing someone else to be present during a meeting is unacceptable to me. I will meet with you only when someone of my choosing is allowed to be present."

- If your adult child is taking items from your home and not returning them:

  "You took my necklace a week ago without permission. I have told you twice that it needs to be returned to me. It must be in my hands tomorrow by 5 p.m., or I will report it stolen."

Remember this vital point: If someone continues disrespecting your boundary, it doesn't mean you didn't have the right to or shouldn't have set that boundary. That is more a reflection of that person than you. Also, keep in mind that "no" is a complete sentence. You have the right to say no at any time, for any reason. You don't need to explain why you said no. That is your business.

Copyright © 2024 Sarkis Media LLC, *A Clinician's Guide to Gaslighting*. All rights reserved.

How to Set Boundaries with Flying Monkeys

When you go no-contact or low-contact with a gaslighter, other people might tell you that the gaslighter misses you and that you should open up the doors of communication again. If you were in a romantic relationship with the gaslighter, the third party may ask if you are seeing someone else and wonder what "really" happened in your relationship. Be aware that the gaslighter may have sent this person to get information from you or to hoover you back into the relationship. This person is known as a "flying monkey," after the Wicked Witch of the West's messengers in *The Wizard of Oz*. Some flying monkeys know that they are transmitting messages from the gaslighter, while some have been unknowingly manipulated into doing so.

Either way, it is crucial to set boundaries with flying monkeys to let them know that the gaslighter is not to be a topic of conversation. Ways to say this include:

- "I'd rather we focus on other things."

- "That's a 'no-fly zone' for me."

- "I don't feel comfortable talking about that person."

- "That's information I'd rather keep to myself."

- "Let's talk about something else."

If a flying monkey continues to bring up the gaslighter, you may need to use the "broken record" technique, where you repeat your original statement until the person drops the subject. If they continue pressuring you, you may need to end the conversation and walk away. It is difficult to do this, but any information you give a flying monkey can cause a cycle of abuse to reignite.

Copyright © 2024 Sarkis Media LLC, *A Clinician's Guide to Gaslighting*. All rights reserved.

Should You Contact the Gaslighter's New Partner?

If you don't go no-contact with a gaslighter after your relationship ends, you may get bombarded with photos of them and their new partner on social media. When this happens, you may be tempted to contact their new partner to warn them about your ex. You may feel like they deserve to know they are setting themselves up to get hurt.

Before you act on this impulse, it's important to remember that gaslighters often describe all their exes as "crazy." There's a good chance the gaslighter is saying the same thing about you to their new partner. As a result, you may contact the latest partner only for them to think (or even tell you), "Oh, my partner warned me that their ex is unstable and would reach out to me."

Sometimes people need to find out about the gaslighter's toxic behaviors on their own. It is not your job to inform your ex's new partner, nor is it your responsibility. It is much more important to work on your healing. Sometimes when you focus on someone else's potential difficulties, it's a way to procrastinate working on your own issues. By contacting your ex's new partner, you are also opening the door to your ex contacting you again. That is something you don't want in your life.

Setting Boundaries When the Gaslighter Contacts You

When working with victims of gaslighting, there may be times when you are contacted by a client's gaslighter, whether it is the client's parent, their significant other, or another person in their life. Usually, you will receive a voicemail, email, or text stating one of the following:

- "I know [*client*] is seeing you for therapy, and I don't think they are giving you the whole story."

- "There are some things I think you need to know about [*client*]."

- "[*Client*] is known for exaggerating and manipulating therapists."

- "[*Client*] lies, and you shouldn't believe what they say."

The gaslighter is concerned that they are being exposed and that the trauma bond is being broken. You may find that their message starts fairly straightforward and coherent and then devolves into word salad or narcissistic rage. Although your client may have previously signed a release of information allowing you to talk to this person, that release may have been signed under duress. Just because you have a release signed by a client does not mean you must communicate with this person.

The best way to proceed is to inform your client that this person has contacted you. Ask your client if they want to see the text, listen to the voicemail, or have you read it. By giving this opportunity to your client, you are enforcing the importance of building autonomy and independence. You can also recommend that your client rescind their release of information, which is another powerful way to enforce boundaries.

When Your Client Requests a Joint Session with a Gaslighter

If your client requests a joint session with the gaslighter in their life (or if they ask you whether you recommend doing so), know that it is generally not recommended to invite a gaslighting or otherwise abusive person to attend a session with your client. A gaslighter will rarely admit to their dysfunctional behaviors and will most likely try to charm you during the session and get you on their side. Less experienced therapists may even be unwittingly pulled into using fawning behaviors to appease the gaslighter.

Instead, ask your client what they hope to achieve from such a session. Let them know that rarely does a gaslighter admit wrongdoing. Your client may be looking for validation that the abuse happened or seeking closure to the relationship. They may also be experiencing an understandable need to punish this person or have you witness the abusive behavior to validate their experiences. Again, the root of many of these needs comes from validation. Look for ways to validate your client's experience further and discuss creating physical distance between your client and their gaslighter if this has not been covered already.

You can also use this as an opportunity to enforce healthy boundaries by giving your client permission to distance themselves from the gaslighter. This empowers them to prioritize their well-being and protect themselves from further manipulation or gaslighting. Discuss the importance of setting clear communication boundaries with the gaslighter, establishing limits on the topics that can be discussed, and creating a plan for disengaging from interactions that become emotionally manipulative or abusive. Working collaboratively with your client, you can help them navigate the challenges of setting boundaries with the gaslighter and support them in their journey toward healing and self-empowerment.

CHAPTER 9

Gaslighting in Organizations

What makes people vulnerable to individual gaslighters also makes them vulnerable to gaslighting at the organizational or group level, such as in their workplace or in a cult. When a client has added social pressure from coworkers, employers, or organization members, the messages they receive about their reality not being "correct" can be even more difficult to escape or process. The tools in this chapter will help you teach clients how to identify instances of workplace harassment, keep written documentation of these instances (and report them accordingly), and navigate making a career change if the harassment continues. You will also learn about group psychological abuse, which can occur when clients are part of cults or similar organizations, such as doomsday or destructive cults. You will discover how to identify whether your client has been a cult member and how to best approach therapy with a client who has recently left a cult or is considering leaving one.

Gaslighting in the Workplace

Gaslighting is a form of workplace harassment, which the U.S. Equal Employment Opportunity Commission (EEOC) defines as "unwelcome conduct that is based on race, color, religion, sex (including sexual orientation, gender identity, or pregnancy), national origin, older age (beginning at age 40), disability, or genetic information (including family medical history)."

Unfortunately, gaslighting in the workplace is a common phenomenon that can take many forms and be perpetrated by a variety of professionals, including colleagues, supervisors, and higher-level management. Here are a few examples of gaslighting behaviors that may occur in a work setting:

- **Denying or undermining achievements:** A gaslighter may downplay or dismiss an employee's accomplishments, making them doubt their competence or contributions to the organization. They may attribute the employee's successes to luck or external factors while loudly praising another employee's accomplishments due to their hard work and intelligence.

- **Withholding information:** Gaslighters may intentionally withhold important information or exclude an employee from crucial discussions or decisions. By keeping them in the dark, they create a sense of confusion and powerlessness, making the employee question their value and worth in the organization. The gaslighter will deny that they withheld information or excluded the employee, even when presented with evidence to the contrary.

- **Shifting blame:** Gaslighters often manipulate situations to make others believe their victim is responsible for mistakes or failures, even when it's not the case. They may twist facts, distort events, or point fingers at others, creating a false narrative that undermines the victim's credibility and self-esteem. If a gaslighter knows a coworker has a cognitive disability, they may blame that person, knowing their victim will be even more vulnerable to others' negative judgments.

- **Creating a hostile or toxic work environment:** Gaslighters may engage in behaviors that contribute to a hostile or toxic work environment, such as constant criticism, humiliation, or belittlement. They may create a culture of fear and intimidation, making it difficult for employees to thrive and succeed.

Gaslighting is most likely to take root in workplace environments with specific characteristics and dynamics. While every situation is unique, the following conditions can create a climate that is conducive to gaslighting:

- **Authoritarian or hierarchical power structures:** Workplace cultures that prioritize hierarchy and exert power differentials between employees can create opportunities for gaslighting. When there is an imbalance of power, individuals in positions of authority may exploit their influence to manipulate and control others.

- **Lack of accountability and transparency:** When organizations lack mechanisms for accountability and transparency, it becomes easier for gaslighters to engage in deceptive behaviors without consequences. This lack of transparency can include secretive decision-making processes, a lack of clear communication channels, or inadequate systems for addressing concerns and grievances.

- **Competitive or cutthroat culture:** Work environments that foster intense competition, where individuals are pitted against each other, can create fertile ground for gaslighting. In such settings, gaslighters may use manipulation tactics to undermine their colleagues' confidence, sabotage their progress, or gain an advantage. Gaslighters see the world as made up of "winners" and "losers" and will resort to any behavior that results in them gaining more power or attention.

- **Absence of psychological safety:** Psychological safety refers to a work environment where employees feel safe to express their thoughts, opinions, and concerns without fear of reprisal. When psychological safety is lacking, employees may be more vulnerable to gaslighting, as they fear the consequences of speaking up or challenging the status quo. Employees who do speak out may be demoted or fired in retaliation.

- **Ineffective leadership and management:** Poor leadership and management practices can contribute to a culture of gaslighting. When leaders fail to model respectful and supportive behavior, exhibit manipulative tendencies, or brush problematic behavior under the rug, it can set the tone for increased gaslighting behaviors within the organization. Ineffective leadership can become enabling behavior when a company discovers an employee's gaslighting behavior and fails to enforce consequences.

Gaslighting can continue in the workplace when it is reinforced and condoned by other employees, coworkers, and managers (Adkins, 2019). Often, clients who experience gaslighting at work are not only being victimized by an individual but are also subjected to mass support of this gaslighting from others in the workplace. This enabling behavior can lead your client to feel betrayed and experience profound grief. Whistle-blowers in the workplace are particularly at risk of being traumatized by institutional gaslighting (Ahern, 2018). Those in power who have no qualms about hurting others can act vengefully toward whistle-blowers who speak out about damaging behaviors. A gaslighter who is called out on their behavior, especially in a public forum, tends to "punish" victims.

Your client has avenues to pursue if they have experienced harassment at work. The first recommendation is that your client meet with an attorney who specializes in employee rights and has particular experience in harassment cases. An attorney can let your client know their rights in the workplace and what next steps they can take, which may include when and how to report the harassment. Here are specific ways an attorney can help:

- **Legal consultation:** An attorney can comprehensively assess your client's situation, review any relevant documentation or evidence, and offer legal advice tailored to their circumstances. They can inform your client about the applicable laws, regulations, and legal protections related to workplace harassment.

- **Rights and remedies:** The attorney can educate your client about their rights as an employee and the potential legal remedies available to them. Legal remedies may include filing a formal complaint with the appropriate administrative agencies, pursuing legal action against the harasser or the employer, or seeking financial compensation for damages.

- **Negotiation and settlement:** The attorney can negotiate your client's case if your client wishes to pursue a resolution outside of court. Their attorney can also speak with them as to whether a settlement may be in their best interest. They can work toward a settlement agreement that provides appropriate compensation, implements workplace changes, and ensures the client's well-being.

- **Legal representation:** If litigation becomes necessary, the attorney can represent your client throughout the legal process. They can prepare and file legal documents, gather evidence, interview witnesses, and present the client's case in court. Having an experienced attorney by their side can significantly enhance your client's chances of achieving a favorable outcome.

Ultimately, your client may need to leave their job and rebuild their career, which is unfair but is in your client's best interest so they can maintain their quality of life.

Have You Experienced Workplace Harassment?

Even individuals in the helping profession aren't immune from workplace harassment. To better help clients, you must explore and come to terms with your own workplace victimization experiences.

Have you ever felt gaslighted, belittled, bullied, or abused in other ways at work? Describe your experience.

_____

_____

_____

_____

How did you respond at the time?

_____

_____

_____

_____

What impact does the harassment have on you today?

_____

_____

_____

_____

Without disclosing your own experiences, how can you use your experiences to help clients who are experiencing harassment at work?

_____

_____

_____

_____

Copyright © 2024 Sarkis Media LLC, *A Clinician's Guide to Gaslighting*. All rights reserved.

Are You Experiencing Gaslighting at Work?

The following scenarios are all examples of gaslighting that constitute workplace harassment. Not only are these situations unethical, but some are also illegal. To determine whether you have experienced gaslighting at work, put a check mark by any situations that apply to you.

❏ You have been given due dates for assignments, only to be told later that you misunderstood the deadline.

❏ Items have been moved on your desk or gone missing while you are out. When you have mentioned it to others, they denied it or told you that you were causing drama.

❏ Someone has told you that other office colleagues are saying you are crazy.

❏ Someone has taken credit for your work on an assignment.

❏ A leader has held a team meeting where you are the only person in attendance.

❏ You have been given a poor performance review after meeting (and sometimes exceeding) your job responsibilities.

❏ You have been told that you didn't complete a task when you did.

❏ Your boss has told you that your team was working late, but you quickly discovered that you were the only one doing so.

❏ Someone in the office has brushed against you as they walk by or "bumped" into you and later denied that it happened.

❏ Someone has quietly made rude comments to you while smiling so no one suspects what they are saying.

❏ You have been left out of team meetings or lunches and told that these gatherings never happened.

❏ You have disclosed a disability to Human Resources, and your boss has told you that you would be a great employee if only you didn't have this disability.

❏ You have been purposefully called into a large meeting after telling your employer that speaking in meetings gives you anxiety or panic attacks.

❏ You have rejected a coworker's advances, only for them to tell you that they were just being friendly.

❏ You have been put on committees and projects with someone you previously reported to your employer for harassment. When you complained, you were told to "tough it out."

Copyright © 2024 Sarkis Media LLC, *A Clinician's Guide to Gaslighting*. All rights reserved.

❑ You have not been paid for overtime hours, while your employer denies you worked overtime.

❑ When you have asked for directives to be put in writing to you, your employer has refused and said that everyone else doesn't need things in writing.

❑ Your employer claims that comments made in the employee feedback portal are anonymous, but you have been called out for your comments and told you are "overreacting."

❑ You have evidence that someone in the office has been accessing your devices. When you've reported it, you've been told that you are delusional.

❑ If you work from home, you have been accused of "not working as hard as people in the office."

❑ At online meetings, you have chosen not to turn on your camera and later been told that you didn't attend the meeting.

If you find that any of these situations apply to you, look at your employee handbook (if you were given one) to see the process for filing a harassment complaint with Human Resources (HR). If you work at a smaller company, there may not be an HR department, so consult an attorney who specializes in employee rights. You can also visit www.eeoc.gov/harassment to see what constitutes workplace harassment.

Copyright © 2024 Sarkis Media LLC, *A Clinician's Guide to Gaslighting*. All rights reserved.

Documenting Gaslighting in the Workplace

If you are experiencing gaslighting or other forms of harassment in your workplace, it is important to keep documentation of the incidents. Make sure to keep your information on a non-employer-owned device because if you quit or are fired, your employer may immediately take the device from you and block you from your company account and cloud-based storage. Your employer may also be able to access activity on your device, even if you have erased it. Therefore, consider keeping your documentation on a privately-owned device in an encrypted file (i.e., password protected).

When documenting these events, make sure to include the following information:

- The date and time an incident occurred

- The person involved and names of any witnesses

- What exactly was said and by whom (including any direct comments in quotation marks)

- Any obscene or threatening nonverbal gestures the person made to you or someone else who was present

- What immediately preceded the event

- Any emotions you experienced during and after the event (guilt, shame, anger, sadness)

If you report the harassment to your HR department, they may want you to give them this documentation. It is best to consult an attorney to determine how to proceed. Usually, you must complete a form that asks you to describe the harassment in detail.

Copyright © 2024 Sarkis Media LLC, *A Clinician's Guide to Gaslighting.* All rights reserved.

Should I Stay or Should I Go?

It can be a miserable way to live if you are experiencing gaslighting at your workplace. Completing this worksheet can help you determine the best course of action if you are considering leaving your job. To determine how much your job interferes with your quality of life, put a check mark by any of the following statements that apply to you.

- ❐ You are experiencing emotional symptoms (e.g., crying, a feeling of impending doom, hopelessness, rage) because of your work environment.

- ❐ You are experiencing physical symptoms (e.g., nausea, headaches, insomnia, panic attacks) because of your work environment.

- ❐ You wake up with a feeling of dread knowing that you have to go to work.

- ❐ The stress from work is causing difficulties in your relationships.

- ❐ You are experiencing more physical illnesses.

- ❐ You feel disconnected and detached from your work.

- ❐ You have started to use substances or increased substance use.

- ❐ You have significant difficulties concentrating on your work.

- ❐ You experience anxiety attacks or panic attacks due to work.

- ❐ You are directing your frustration or anger toward an innocent person in the office.

- ❐ You are experiencing increased cynicism, believing people are only "out for themselves."

- ❐ You lack motivation or interest in your work.

If you checked off multiple items from this list, you might want to consider taking the necessary steps to find a different job so you can leave this toxic work environment. I also recommend that you meet with an attorney who specializes in employee rights to determine what options are available to you. Bring this worksheet to your consultation session to detail how this situation affects your quality of life. You can also discuss this worksheet with your therapist to determine your next steps.

 Copyright © 2024 Sarkis Media LLC, *A Clinician's Guide to Gaslighting*. All rights reserved.

Guiding Your Client Through New Employment

In a perfect world, the gaslighter in your client's workplace would be fired, and your client would go on to have a drama-free work environment. However, gaslighters may use various tactics to maintain their jobs, such as spreading false information about their colleagues or superiors to create doubt and confusion, manipulating situations to make it appear like others are at fault, aligning themselves with powerful colleagues or superiors, and leveraging their position of authority, such as being a supervisor or manager, to maintain their position without being held accountable.

As a result of gaslighting, your client may be paying a high emotional and physical price to stay in a toxic work environment. When this occurs, you may need to help your client assess the pros and cons of staying at their current job. There are several important factors that your client will want to take into consideration. For example, a pro of staying in a toxic work environment is that it may provide your client with a sense of familiarity and stability. Your client knows what to expect, and there may be a level of comfort in the routine and familiarity with colleagues and tasks. It may also provide a consistent income and financial stability, as leaving a job without having another one lined up can create financial uncertainty. Finally, your client's workplace may offer important opportunities for skill development, especially if the employer pays for certification training or college courses that could benefit your client when they leave their job.

However, there are also cons to consider, the first of which being that a toxic work environment can significantly negatively impact your client's mental and physical well-being. They are likely to experience increased stress, anxiety, burnout, and potential health problems. Remaining in a toxic work environment can also impede learning, innovation, and collaboration, limiting your client's ability to develop new skills and advance in their career. Finally, the adverse effects of a toxic work environment can spread to other areas of your client's life, affecting their personal relationships, self-esteem, and overall happiness. It can be challenging to separate work from other aspects of life.

If the pros of leaving the job outweigh the cons, your client may use this opportunity to make a career change if their current career leaves them feeling depleted, apathetic, and disconnected from their sense of mission or purpose. Your client may also need to switch careers if the gaslighter has successfully "blacklisted" them from their field or your client has a strict noncompete clause. Your client may feel profound grief, anger, and powerlessness over losing a job they have worked hard to find and maintain. It is essential to validate your client's feelings of injustice and to ask if they would like to explore avenues of filing a formal grievance if they have not already done so. As mentioned earlier, consider referring your client to an attorney specializing in employee rights.

If your client needs to make a career switch, consider using a validated occupational assessment tool, such as the RIASEC Interest Inventory (Holland, 1997), to help your client find a new path. The RIASEC Inventory classifies people into six work categories that reflect their natural abilities: realistic, investigative, artistic, social, enterprising, and conventional. Other online career assessments may be available for free or at a low cost that can point your client to a career that reflects their interests and strengths.

Pros and Cons of Making a Career Change

You can use the following chart to consider the advantages and disadvantages of staying in your current workplace versus finding a job elsewhere.

Option	Pros	Cons
Staying at the same job		
Making a career change		

Copyright © 2024 Sarkis Media LLC, *A Clinician's Guide to Gaslighting*. All rights reserved.

Gaslighting in Cults

Victims can be drawn into cults, also known as groups of psychological abuse, through various mechanisms that exploit their vulnerabilities and manipulate their emotional, psychological, and social needs. Cults often target individuals who are seeking answers, purpose, or a sense of belonging. They may offer a seemingly supportive and tight-knit community that promises solutions to personal problems, spiritual enlightenment, or a particular mission or purpose. People experiencing a transition or crisis—who are otherwise vulnerable or searching for meaning in their lives—may be more susceptible to cult recruitment as well. Clients are more vulnerable if they are facing personal or family difficulties, isolation, loss, or a lack of social support.

Once someone is in a cult, the organization will use various tactics to maintain control over the individual's thoughts, emotions, and behaviors. They may use love bombing—showering the victim with excessive attention, flattery, and acts of kindness—to create a sense of indebtedness and dependency. They also employ various mind-control, or thought-stopping, techniques that interrupt critical thinking and create a trance-like state. This can include repetitive chanting, singing, and speaking in tongues. In addition, they often use sleep deprivation, dietary restrictions, meditation practices, and other methods to induce altered consciousness and suggestibility.

Cults gradually introduce and reinforce their belief systems, slowly eroding individual autonomy and critical thinking. They may use group pressure, fear, guilt, or manipulation of personal values to instill loyalty and compliance. This manipulation can make it challenging for victims to question or leave the group without experiencing significant emotional and psychological repercussions. In addition, cults often isolate individuals from their existing support systems to diminish outside influences and increase control over members' lives. They may discourage or prohibit contact with non-members and instill fear or distrust toward outsiders.

The following are all examples of cults or groups of psychological abuse:

- **Destructive cults:** Destructive cults cause severe injury or death to their members or other people. They are characterized by the exploitation and manipulation of individuals for the leader's benefit, often resulting in significant harm to the members' well-being, autonomy, and freedom. For example, in 1978, Jim Jones and the Peoples Temple led a mass murder-suicide that resulted in over 900 deaths.

- **Doomsday cults:** A doomsday cult, also known as an apocalyptic or end-times cult, is an organization that revolves around a belief system centered on an impending catastrophic event or the end of the world. Doomsday cult members typically subscribe to a set of beliefs that include predictions about the imminent destruction, transformation, or salvation of the world or humanity. The leader or leaders of the cult often claim to have special knowledge or divine revelation about the impending doomsday scenario.

- **Racist cults:** Members of a racist cult adhere to and propagate beliefs that assert the superiority or inferiority of individuals based on their racial or ethnic background. The primary focus of a racist cult is to promote and maintain a system of racial discrimination, exclusion, or hatred.

- **Terrorist cults:** The defining factor of a terrorist cult is its utilization of violence, terrorism, or the promotion of violent acts to further its goals. Members of a terrorist cult may engage in acts of violence, including bombings, assassinations, or other forms of targeted attacks. They may justify their actions based on ideological or political motivations, and the group leader often exerts significant control over the decision-making process.

- **Religious cults:** A religious cult is a social group or organization that revolves around a religious or spiritual belief system characterized by distinctive practices, rituals, and doctrines. A religious cult may arise within an already established religion or outside of existing organizations.

- **Political cults:** A political cult is a group or organization that exhibits cult-like characteristics and that revolves around a political ideology or a particular political leader. In a political cult, the leader or leaders hold significant authority and control over the members, often utilizing manipulative tactics to maintain power and loyalty.

- **Polygamist cults:** Members of a polygamist cult are often coerced into entering and maintaining polygamous marriages, with the leader typically holding multiple spouses themselves. Polygamy within these cults may involve significant power imbalances, coercion, and exploitation.

- **Wellness cults:** A wellness cult uses pseudoscience and a promise of health or longevity to lure members. Non-standardized bloodwork inevitably shows a "diagnosis" that can only be helped by expensive and lengthy "treatments." Wellness cults particularly prey upon people who have not found a solution to their symptoms through science-based medical treatment.

- **Multi-level marketing organizations:** The multi-level marketing (MLM) business model can resemble a pyramid scheme, emphasizing recruitment rather than the actual sale of products or services. There have been instances where MLM companies have faced legal scrutiny or allegations of deceptive practices. The leaders often use obfuscation, financial manipulation, and harsh criticism, leading participants to blame themselves for their "failure" to achieve financial success in the scheme.

Although there are many different types of cults, these organizations often share some common traits, particularly with regard to more extremist cults:

- Members are told that they must give a certain amount of money or perform certain acts to become one of the "saved" or "elite."

- A totalitarian system is in place where members are not allowed to have their own opinions.

- There is an embargo against outside media.

- Cult members are rarely left alone.

- There are smaller group "meetings" with an older or more established member who reinforces the cult's beliefs.

- There are strict gender roles.

- Members are punished for questioning the cult or for trying to escape.

- Members are threatened with being ostracized if they leave the cult.

- Members are blackmailed into staying with information procured by the cult.

- There are strata for members, with lower-level members being pressured to rise to the higher ranks.

- Members are given special privileges if they adhere to the cult's strict rules.

- Members are told they must engage in sexual activity with the cult leader.

- There is often human trafficking of lower-ranked members.

- Members are required to shun family and friends outside of the cult.

Although the term *cult* is sometimes used to discredit a group that the speaker disagrees with or a community that is marginalized by the larger society, it's important to note that not all groups or communities labeled as cults are inherently harmful or dangerous. To distinguish a true cult from another type of group, consider whether it exhibits the specific problematic or harmful characteristics noted in the previous list.

If your client recently left a group of psychological abuse, they may be hesitant to speak about the events that characterized their time in the cult, especially given the secret-keeping and forced loyalty required of cult members. They may even have been led to believe that sharing this information will harm them or their family members. Your client may meet the diagnostic criteria for PTSD due to the abuse they experienced in the cult. Given these circumstances, therapy may take longer than it would with other traumatic issues. Emphasize how brave it was for your client to attend therapy, and take your time building rapport. You may be one of only a handful of people outside the cult to whom the client has spoken. Work at the client's pace, getting to know your client's likes, dislikes, and interests separate from talking about the cult.

Once you have established rapport, it is completely expected for your client to bring up "surface" issues currently happening in their life. For example, they may discuss a roommate issue characterizing their new living arrangement. Your client is waiting to see how you react to these comparatively minor problems before they delve deeper into their traumatic experiences. Refrain from speaking about the cult or pushing them to disclose the abuse or trauma they experienced. Although you may feel like this is the best way to help your client, you risk them shutting down and discontinuing therapy if your agenda takes over.

Could You Be the Victim of a Cult or Other Gaslighting Organization?

Read through the following list and check off any items that apply to your organization, even if they have only appeared briefly.

☐ Are there rules that only certain members need to follow?

☐ Does the organization lack a governing body or system that would check leaders' use of power?

☐ Are concerns and complaints met with accusations that you are not being "faithful" or "good"?

☐ Are the organization's budget and process for money management kept secret from most members?

☐ Is the leader seen as having special powers?

☐ Is there a division between "lower" and "higher" members?

☐ Is your status in the organization based on how much money you donate?

☐ Are you told that people outside of the organization are evil?

☐ Do you suspect there is a history of sexual abuse in the organization that is being perpetrated by those in power?

☐ Are you punished for not following the organization's rules?

☐ Are you told that you must cut off contact with friends and family who aren't organization members?

☐ When you say you want to leave the organization, are you guilted, shamed, or blackmailed into staying?

☐ Are you told that bad things will happen to people you love if you leave the organization?

☐ Are you told that you will be shunned if you leave the organization?

☐ Are members told that only certain people can attain a "pure" or "good" status?

☐ Are the organization's rules rigid and unable to be changed for any reason?

☐ Are the decisions of the organization made only by one or two people?

☐ Have family or friends told you that they are concerned for your well-being?

☐ Is there a requirement that members must live together?

☐ Are you watched or monitored by the organization?

☐ Are you told that family and friends outside the organization aren't allowed to visit you?

☐ Is mental health treatment viewed as untrustworthy and actively discouraged?

If you answered yes to any of these questions, you might be a member of a cult or other gaslighting organization. Please show this list to your therapist to discuss possible next steps.

Copyright © 2024 Sarkis Media LLC, *A Clinician's Guide to Gaslighting*. All rights reserved.

**Client
Handout**

Coping with a Family Member Who Is in a Cult

When a family member is in a situation that is not healthy for them, it can be heartbreaking. You may spend sleepless nights wondering how you can help them. The situation can get even more complicated if your family member is in a cult or other gaslighting organization. Any attempts to convince your loved one that they are in an unhealthy situation may cause them to become even more attached to the organization. Cults have built-in "scripts" for dissuading victims from leaving. They have an answer prepared for every reason that victims give for wanting to leave the cult. Common gaslighting statements cult leaders use include:

- "Your family doesn't know what is best for you, and they never have."

- "Of course they want you to leave; you are finally happy."

- "You'll never attain [*salvation, a higher status, etc.*] if you leave. Our way is the only way."

- "You'll never have freedom again."

Cult members may also be threatened or blackmailed into staying. Unfortunately, unless your loved one tells you they are being harmed or held against their will, there is little law enforcement can do. While you can ask for a welfare check, your loved one may claim that everything is okay if they meet with law enforcement in the presence of another cult member. You must tell law enforcement that your loved one needs to be spoken to alone, without a cult member present.

Above all, your loved one will likely not leave the cult until they are ready to go. A cult member may be prepared to leave when:

- They initiate or increase contact with you.

- The cult leader is charged with a crime or multiple crimes.

- The cult is moving to a distant location.

- They can no longer afford to stay in the cult.

- They obtain access to outside media and read about the cult.

Until then, the most important thing you can do is practice good self-care. Nurture yourself and your relationships with others. Some couples find that having a family member in a cult can cause a significant strain on their relationship, particularly when each partner has a different preferred plan of action, so consider attending couples therapy.

The best thing you can do for your loved one is to not enable them financially, such as by depositing money into their bank account or giving them cash, as you may be inadvertently supporting the cult. Financially cutting off a family member is a difficult decision, and it is normal to feel guilty. Let your loved one know that when they decide to leave, you will welcome them back with open arms, no questions asked. You can't fix the situation, but you can provide support.

CHAPTER 10

Self-Care

Self-care is an essential part of healing from a gaslighter. When a person is in a toxic relationship, they are made to feel as if their wants and needs aren't important, while the gaslighter's wants and needs are made paramount. If the victim makes any attempts to put themselves first, this is met with guilting and shaming by their abuser. As a result, victims of gaslighting are led to believe that self-care is a luxury born out of selfishness instead of embracing it as a right. They may find themselves out of balance and only engage in self-care when they reach a breaking point.

Part of your role as a clinician is to orient your client toward proactive self-care. With proactive self-care, your client regularly takes care of their physical and emotional health so that when difficulties arise, they feel more resilient and have more strategies at their disposal. Proactive self-care is in contrast to reactive self-care, which is done only in response to a crisis or chronic stress. In this chapter, you will explore various proactive self-care strategies that clients can practice, including journaling, mindfulness meditation, healthy eating and sleeping habits, and affirmations.

Proactive Versus Reactive Self-Care

If you have a gaslighter in your life, you may have been told you were selfish whenever you prioritized your own needs. (Meanwhile, the gaslighter put themselves first all the time.) They may even have told you that you weren't a good person if you practiced self-care. However, the reality is that self-care is essential to your well-being. You must tend to yourself to maintain your physical, emotional, and mental health.

There are two kinds of self-care: reactive and proactive. Reactive self-care is the kind you engage in only after reaching a crisis point or burnout. Examples of reactive self-care include only meditating when you are stressed out, intensely exercising when you aren't feeling good about your body, or waiting for an urgent medical issue to see your doctor instead of getting regular checkups.

In contrast, proactive self-care involves caring for yourself before a crisis hits. Proactive self-care is the best way to protect your physical, emotional, and mental well-being so you don't burn out. In proactive self-care, you take time out each day to self-reflect or do something that gives you joy or recharges you. Examples of proactive self-care include regularly going to therapy, getting some physical movement every day, journaling, communicating your wants and needs, and consistently reviewing your life and career to see if you are where you want to be.

Copyright © 2024 Sarkis Media LLC, *A Clinician's Guide to Gaslighting*. All rights reserved.

Self-Care Checklist

The following are some quick and easily accessible ways you can practice self-care. The best options are ones that are inexpensive and require no extra equipment. Put a check mark by any activities you already incorporate into your routine and circle any activities you'd like to try.

- ❒ Go for a walk
- ❒ Cuddle with a pet
- ❒ Write in a journal
- ❒ Put together a puzzle
- ❒ Eat a snack
- ❒ Do some deep breathing
- ❒ Listen to a guided meditation
- ❒ Take a bath or shower
- ❒ Do a craft, like crochet
- ❒ Play with your kids
- ❒ Watch a show or movie
- ❒ Get a massage or give yourself one
- ❒ Take an exercise class
- ❒ Listen to music
- ❒ Do some gardening

- ❒ Read a book or article
- ❒ Paint, draw, or color
- ❒ Take a short nap
- ❒ Write down what you are grateful for
- ❒ Name three things you can see, three things you can hear, and three things you can feel
- ❒ Play a musical instrument
- ❒ Play a board game
- ❒ Stretch
- ❒ Give yourself a manicure or pedicure
- ❒ Write down three positive qualities about yourself
- ❒ Call or text a trusted friend
- ❒ Practice a skin care routine
- ❒ Do some yoga
- ❒ Other: _____

Self-Care Check-In

To help you understand the importance of self-care, try this quick self-care check-in every day. To begin, consider a scale from 1 to 10, where 1 is the worst you've felt and 10 is the best you've felt. What number are you at on the scale right now?

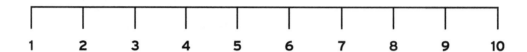

1   2   3   4   5   6   7   8   9   10

Look through the previous *Self-Care Checklist* and identify one strategy to enhance your score on this scale. Take time to practice this strategy now, then use the same scale to rate your feelings afterward.

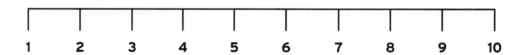

1   2   3   4   5   6   7   8   9   10

Chances are, you'll find that your score on this scale improves, even if just by one number. Check in with yourself every day to complete this exercise. You may even find it helpful to check in more than once a day or whenever you are aware of increased stress levels. You can use the log on the following page to keep track of your ratings before and after you practice self-care.

Copyright © 2024 Sarkis Media LLC, *A Clinician's Guide to Gaslighting.* All rights reserved.

Self-Care Log

Date/Time	Self-Care Practice	Rating Before (1-10)	Rating After (1-10)

Copyright © 2024 Sarkis Media LLC, *A Clinician's Guide to Gaslighting.* All rights reserved.

Do a Body Scan

When a gaslighter has told you that what you think and feel doesn't matter, you may respond by numbing your emotions and ignoring signs of stress. You may have reached a point where you aren't feeling much of anything, including physical symptoms such as hunger or tiredness. It's essential to get back in touch with how your body feels. When you are connected to your body's internal cues, you can take care of your needs when they arise. Otherwise, you delay your self-care, which can lead to burnout and even suicidal thoughts.

Use the figure to label how stress shows up in different parts of your body. Many people report that when they feel stressed or anxious, it shows up as:

- Headaches

- Numbness in the hands

- Increased sweating

- Racing heartbeat

- Thoughts of doom

When you start feeling these indicators of stress or anxiety, practice a self-care strategy from *the Self-Care Checklist*.

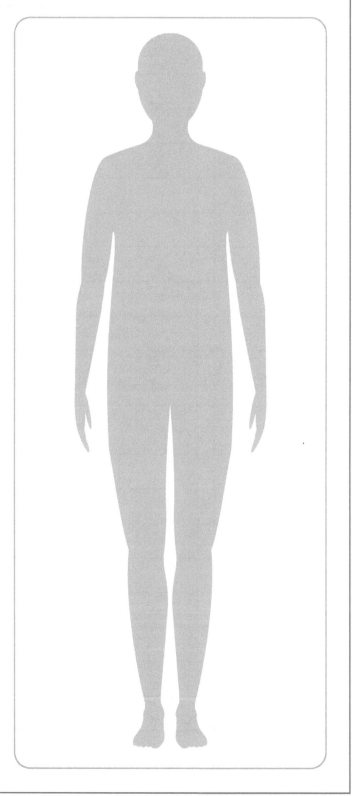

Copyright © 2024 Sarkis Media LLC, *A Clinician's Guide to Gaslighting*. All rights reserved.

Mindfulness

At its core, mindfulness is about nonjudgmentally and intentionally being with the present moment as it is, right here, right now. When some clients think of mindfulness, they picture themselves sitting still or lying down and trying to empty their minds. Although mindfulness can involve formal practices, such as meditation, it can also involve informal practices that clients can incorporate into routine parts of their day. For example, clients can practice mindfulness when eating, driving, or showering—simply bringing their full attention to the experience of each activity. For many clients, informal mindfulness practices are more user-friendly and, therefore, more effective in helping them quiet their thoughts and center their minds. It is one of the most straightforward and accessible forms of self-care.

When talking to your clients about mindfulness, ask them what they already know. There can be a wide range of experiences with mindfulness, from clients who have heard about it in passing to clients who practice it several times a day. For some clients, mindfulness can be a part of their religious practice, though it is not a religious practice in itself. For example, some clients may regularly engage in prayer, a form of meditative practice. Other clients may have an affirmation they often repeat to themselves, which is another form of mindfulness.

The following are some simple and accessible mindfulness practices that you might encourage clients to incorporate into their routine:

- Body scan
- Mindful eating
- Walking meditation
- Deep breathing

In the following handouts, you'll find sample scripts for mindful breathing and eating practices. Since the goal of mindfulness is to be present in the here and now, whatever healthy way your client wants to achieve this is acceptable. Reinforce that they can choose what mindfulness practices work best for them, based on their environment, daily schedule, and opportunities to spend time alone. Financial means should not play a role in accessing mindfulness.

Mindful Breathing

This mindful breathing practice can bring you a feeling of calm and peacefulness. To begin, find a comfortable seated position with your feet planted on the ground and your spine straight but relaxed. Gently close your eyes or soften your gaze.

Take a moment to bring your awareness to your breath. Notice the sensation of the breath as it enters and leaves your body. Feel the natural rhythm of your breath without trying to change it.

Now, bring your attention to your nostrils. As you inhale, feel the coolness of the air entering your nostrils. And as you exhale, feel the warmth of the breath leaving your nostrils. Observe this sensation without judgment or interpretation.

As you continue to breathe, begin to deepen your breath. Take a slow, deep breath through your nose, allowing your belly to expand fully. Then exhale slowly through your nose, allowing your stomach to contract gently. Take a few more deep breaths this way, focusing on the sensation of the breath filling and emptying your body.

Now, shift your attention to your chest. Notice the gentle rise and fall of your chest with each breath. Feel the expansion of your ribcage as you inhale and the softening of your chest as you exhale. Stay present with this movement, letting go of any distractions or thoughts that may arise.

Next, bring your awareness to your entire body. Feel your breath flowing through your body, nourishing every cell. With each out-breath, imagine any tension or stress melting away and a sense of relaxation spreading through your body.

If your mind starts to wander or thoughts arise, acknowledge them without judgment and gently guide your attention back to your breath. Use your breath as an anchor to keep you grounded in the present moment.

Take a few more moments to continue this mindful breathing practice, allowing yourself to fully relax and be present with each breath.

When you're ready, slowly bring your attention back to your surroundings. Gently wiggle your fingers and toes, then open your eyes.

You can return to this mindful breathing practice whenever you need to find a moment of calm and presence in your day.

Copyright © 2024 Sarkis Media LLC, *A Clinician's Guide to Gaslighting*. All rights reserved.

Mindful Eating

This mindful eating practice can guide you through a more conscious and present experience with your food. Begin by selecting a piece of food, such as a small fruit or a bite-sized snack. Take a moment to observe its shape, color, and texture. Notice any sensations that arise as you hold it in your hand.

Bring the food closer to your nose and take a deep breath, inhaling its aroma. Notice any scents or fragrances that you can detect.

Now, slowly bring the food to your mouth but resist biting. Pause for a moment and observe any physical sensations or anticipation that arises within you.

When you're ready, take a small bite of the food. Pay attention to the flavors and textures that you experience. Notice how the food feels against your tongue and teeth. Take your time to chew slowly and deliberately, savoring each moment.

As you continue to chew, bring your full attention to the taste of the food. Notice the different flavors that emerge—the sweetness, the bitterness, or the savory notes. Explore the nuances of the taste and allow yourself to experience it fully.

As you swallow the bite, feel the sensation of the food moving down your throat and into your stomach. Take a moment to acknowledge the nourishment it provides to your body.

Pause for a moment before taking another bite. Observe any sensations or thoughts that arise during this pause. Notice if you desire to rush or eat quickly, and gently bring your attention back to the present moment.

Continue to eat mindfully, bite by bite, fully engaging your senses in the experience. Take the time to appreciate the food and the nourishment it offers. Allow yourself to be fully present with each bite, free from distractions or rushing.

If your mind wanders or you find yourself getting lost in thoughts, bring your focus back to the sensations of eating. You can also use your breath as an anchor to bring you back to the present moment.

As you near the end of this mindful eating practice, take a moment to reflect on the experience. Notice any changes in your awareness or connection with your food. Consider how this practice might translate to your everyday meals.

When you're ready, gently conclude the practice and take a moment to express gratitude for the food and the nourishment it provides. Remember, you can incorporate mindful eating into your daily meals by bringing more awareness to the present moment, savoring each bite, and cultivating a deeper connection with your food.

Physical Self-Care: Exercise, Sleep, and Eating Habits

Exercise

Victims of gaslighting can benefit significantly from engaging in a regular exercise routine, which is one of the most effective ways to reduce stress and anxiety. Although it is generally recommended that people get at least 150 minutes of moderate physical activity per week, research shows that even 10 minutes of moderate to vigorous exercise one to two days a week can help people cope with challenging situations (Nakagawa et al., 2020). Exercise may also play a significant role in disrupting the biochemical effects of the trauma bond because it triggers the release of endorphins, which act as mood enhancers and pain relievers. Therefore, encourage your clients to get some form of exercise or movement during the day, whether they want to dance to music or hop on a treadmill. Importantly, your client does not need to engage in vigorous exercise to reap the benefits of movement—it can be as simple as doing gentle yoga, stretching, or walking. There is also a healing component to spending time outside, so encourage them to get outdoors as much as possible.

If your client feels overwhelmed at the thought of starting an exercise regimen, encourage them to start with more manageable steps, such as moving their body for just 15 minutes per day. You also want to remind them that action precedes motivation. In other words, they can get up and move even if they don't feel motivated. Sometimes the inspiration will come once your client has started moving their body in a way that feels enjoyable.

Sleep

The chronic stress caused by gaslighting can lead to disturbed sleep patterns, even in clients who previously slept well. Ask your client about their sleep habits and whether they feel rested in the morning. Not only can sleep deprivation affect your client's mood, but it can also affect brain function and impair decision-making. Therefore, make sure to ask your client the following questions at their initial evaluation:

- How much sleep do you get on an average night?
- Do you feel refreshed or tired when you wake up?
- Do you use an app or watch to track your sleep?
- Do you have frequent nightmares? If so, how often do they wake you up?
- Do you have a hard time falling asleep?
- Do you wake up in the middle of the night for no reason?
- Do you wake up too early and have trouble falling back asleep?
- Do you fall asleep while watching TV?
- Do you snore?
- Do you take any medications or supplements to help you sleep?

Any of these signs could indicate a sleep disturbance, which can be related to inherited sleep patterns, stress, sleep apnea or other medical conditions, medications, hunger or food insecurity, and more. Your client may also have been conditioned into poor sleep habits, as the gaslighter may have tormented them by keeping them awake at night, leading to hypervigilance. A primary care provider or psychiatrist may prescribe a sleep study to your client to determine whether any medical issues could be contributing to a lack of sleep.

Eating Habits

Clients, particularly those with a history of disordered eating, can have exacerbated issues with food when they are in a gaslighting relationship. It is common for gaslighters to criticize other people's eating habits and body types, especially if they know this is an area in which the other person is particularly vulnerable. Some gaslighting victims have even been prevented from accessing healthy food or food necessary for their well-being because the gaslighter told them they were overweight. They may continue to avoid or restrict certain foods or, on the other end of the spectrum, use food as a coping mechanism.

For clients to heal their relationship with food, it can be helpful for them to learn the principles of intuitive eating—honoring their hunger cues, practicing mindful eating, rejecting the diet mentality, and appreciating their body regardless of its appearance. If you don't specialize in eating disorders or intuitive eating, consider consulting a clinician with that expertise. You might also consider referring your client to a registered dietitian if they demonstrate signs of disordered eating or have medical conditions that necessitate a particular diet. Depending on the severity of their disordered eating habits, you may need to refer your client to a treatment center.

Discover Ways You Can Get Exercise

As little as 10 minutes of moderate to vigorous exercise can boost your brain's "feel-good" chemicals. It can also enhance the part of your brain responsible for mood regulation, self-control, reasoning, and many other processes that help you make better decisions. You don't need a strenuous workout routine to get enough exercise. Taking the stairs instead of the elevator, parking farther away from your office, or having a dance party with your kids all count as exercise. Put a check mark by any types of exercise that you already incorporate into your routine, and circle any forms of movement you'd be interested in trying out.

❒ Dancing

❒ Swimming

❒ Weightlifting or resistance training

❒ Jumping rope

❒ Martial arts

❒ Bodyweight exercises

❒ Yoga

❒ Playing actively with kids or pets

❒ Jumping at the trampoline park

❒ Indoor rock climbing

❒ Hiking

❒ Cycling or spinning

❒ Soccer

❒ Gardening or yard work

❒ Kayaking or canoeing

❒ Rollerblading

❒ Stretching

❒ Balance exercises

❒ Sitting on an exercise ball

❒ Boxing

❒ Virtual reality or other exercise apps

❒ Walking

❒ Aqua aerobics

❒ Pilates

❒ Golf or mini-golf

❒ Other: _____

Copyright © 2024 Sarkis Media LLC, *A Clinician's Guide to Gaslighting*. All rights reserved.

Good Sleep Habits

Not only can sleep deprivation lead to exhaustion, but it also increases feelings of anxiety and depression. In order to practice good sleep hygiene, try to follow these recommendations:

- Go to bed and wake up at the same times, even on weekends.

- Sleep in a completely dark room (unless this triggers trauma).

- Get at least eight hours of sleep each night.

- Shut off electronics at least an hour before bed.

- Sleep in a quiet room or use a noise-canceling device.

- Purchase a new mattress if yours is more than seven years old or feels uncomfortable.

- Engage in a relaxing activity before bed (e.g., light stretching, reading).

- Incorporate exercise or movement into your day and check with your doctor before starting an exercise program.

- Keep your bedroom at a cool temperature (around 65 degrees Fahrenheit).

- If you are prescribed medication to help you sleep, take it before you need to fall asleep. Ask your doctor about appropriate scheduling.

- Avoid caffeine in the afternoon and evening.

- Drink alcohol only in moderation, and avoid eating foods before bedtime that may cause indigestion.

- Use a sleep-tracking watch or app to help you track how much time you are asleep.

- Avoid taking naps, as this can throw off your nighttime sleep (and contrary to what you may have heard, you can't make up for lack of sleep by napping).

Try one of these good sleep habits to see if it changes how you feel when you wake up. If you are getting enough sleep, you should feel refreshed. Talk with your therapist about other ways to get enough sleep.

Client Worksheet

Sleep Journal

Keeping a written sleep record is an alternative to using a sleep-tracking app or watch to monitor your sleep. You might find patterns and behaviors that you can change when you keep a sleep log.

Date	Bedtime	Time to Fall Asleep	Waketime	How You Felt Upon Waking	Daytime Nap? (if yes, note duration)	Symptoms Present Before Bedtime (e.g., stressed, sick, overate, underate, pain, headache, thirsty)

Copyright © 2024 Sarkis Media LLC, *A Clinician's Guide to Gaslighting*. All rights reserved.

Food as a Coping Mechanism

Many people use eating as a way to cope with chronic stress. To determine how much you use food as a coping mechanism, put a check mark by any of the following statements you agree with.

☐   1.   I feel better after I eat carbohydrates or sugary foods.

☐   2.   I never feel completely satisfied when I eat.

☐   3.   I eat while I am doing something else.

☐   4.   I overeat regularly.

☐   5.   I eat quickly.

☐   6.   I eat for reasons other than hunger.

☐   7.   Friends and family have expressed concern about my eating habits.

☐   8.   Food gives me a sense of soothing and calm that I don't get anywhere else.

☐   9.   I have gained over 10 percent of my body weight in the past six months.

☐ 10.   I feel guilt and shame when I feel I have overeaten.

Please share these items with your therapist if you agree with any of these statements. You may be engaging in emotional eating, a common occurrence when people are under great stress. Your therapist can help you learn healthier coping methods and change your relationship with food.

Journaling

Journaling is a powerful tool to help clients process their experiences in a gaslighting relationship. Not only can it reduce the intensity of their anxiety, depression, and PTSD symptoms, but it can also improve overall psychological resilience (Smyth et al., 2018). Remember that gaslighting leaves victims questioning their reality, perceptions, and sanity. Journaling provides a safe and private space for them to write down their encounters, helping to rebuild trust in their perceptions and reclaim their sense of reality. Through journaling, victims can also detect any recurring themes, patterns, triggers, or specific techniques the gaslighter uses. This awareness can help victims recognize the manipulation and regain control over their narrative.

Journaling can take varied forms, depending on what appeals to your client the most. For example, some clients prefer writing about or dictating their experiences, while others may want to put their experiences into a musical or visual form. They can use a self-reflection prompt to summarize their day, journal about what they are thankful for, or engage in stream-of-consciousness journaling, where they write down whatever is on their mind and practice letting go of self-criticism. Any format they choose can be effective. The following are some prompts you can consider giving to your client:

- Through your experience of your relationship with a gaslighter, what have you learned about yourself?

- What have you gained as a result of your relationship with a gaslighter?

- How are you feeling today? What's on your mind? Write about anything that concerns you today.

- If your life was exactly the way you wanted it to be, what would it look like?

- What are you thankful for today?

Positive Affirmations

A positive affirmation is any short phrase or statement your client can repeat to themselves to overcome self-doubt and encourage a positive outlook. Effective affirmations are phrased as declarations of strength, confidence, and positivity. For example, instead of conveying something that your client doesn't want ("I won't entertain negative thoughts"), you can transform the statement into what they do want ("Today, I will choose to think positively"). Other effective affirmations include:

- I am healthy.

- I appreciate my life.

- Positive people surround me.

- I am expecting great things to happen today.

- I am calm and at peace.

- I can handle anything that comes my way.

Affirmations are even more powerful when your client creates their own. They are more likely to own and practice them daily if they are the author. However, if a client has trouble coming up with their own affirmations, you can also provide a list they can choose from. While they may not "buy into" some of these affirmations at first, just repeating the statement to themselves can eventually become a self-fulfilling prophecy.

One of the great things about affirmations is that your client can carry them anywhere. They can put their affirmations on their phone, bathroom mirror, or refrigerator to remind them to repeat these statements throughout the day. They can then "plug in" the affirmation at any point, anywhere, and no one will notice. There is no minimum or maximum number of affirmations your client needs to do in a day—it's whatever feels right to them. They can also decide to change their affirmations. A change may be particularly appropriate when they have reached a milestone in their healing journey.

Creating Your Affirmations

Being in a toxic relationship can make it feel like things are falling apart, especially if you've experienced gaslighting. You have a right to feel good about yourself, and affirmations are an excellent way to achieve that. An affirmation is a brief statement of encouragement or positivity to help you reframe how you want to live and view yourself. Put a check mark by any of the following affirmations that resonate with you.

- ❏ I am resilient and can overcome challenges.

- ❏ I embrace change as a chance for growth.

- ❏ I release the need to compare myself to others.

- ❏ I am capable of setting healthy boundaries that protect my well-being.

- ❏ I deserve love, respect, and kindness from myself and others.

- ❏ I can practice self-compassion, treating myself with kindness and understanding.

- ❏ I trust my intuition and can make choices that align with my values.

- ❏ I embrace my emotions and allow myself to feel them without judgment.

You can also develop your affirmations by thinking of short motivating phrases that remind you of what you want to accomplish in life or what qualities you want to embody. For example, "I can do anything I set my mind to" or "I deserve to feel happy." It's best to keep your affirmations to a short sentence. It also helps to have more than one from which to choose. Write down any affirmations here that you'd like to carry with you.

_____

_____

_____

_____

_____

_____

_____

_____

_____

Copyright © 2024 Sarkis Media LLC, *A Clinician's Guide to Gaslighting*. All rights reserved.

CHAPTER 11

When Your Client Plans to Leave or Has Left

The most dangerous—and potentially lethal—time for your client is when they are planning to leave the gaslighter or have just left the abusive relationship. Emotional abuse is just one part of domestic violence; when there is gaslighting in a relationship, there is a much greater chance of physical abuse. There are several reasons why this is the case. First, abusers like to exert power and control in relationships, and the thought of losing that control can trigger intense feelings of anger, frustration, and desperation. Second, when a victim leaves, the gaslighter experiences a narcissistic injury and may take extreme measures to regain control. Third, the victim may no longer be willing to hide the abuse upon leaving, and the gaslighter may fear the consequences of being exposed to others.

In this chapter, you will learn how to discover your client's ultimate limits in a gaslighting relationship: the limits that push them to leave their abuser. In particular, you will uncover where your client draws the line in a gaslighting relationship and learn the components of a safety plan so that your client can protect themselves and their loved ones, such as children or pets. Given the potential dangers of leaving an abusive relationship, victims must seek support from clinicians, domestic violence shelters, hotlines, and legal resources to help them navigate the complex process of leaving their abuser.

You will also learn about the types of threats that gaslighters make to their victims and how to determine when your client should consider filing for a restraining order or injunction so they can protect themselves from further abuse. Finally, you will learn the challenges of coparenting with a gaslighter, what questions your client should ask a family law attorney, what a detailed parenting plan looks like, and the importance of using a coparenting app as the primary form of communication with a gaslighter.

Where Does Your Client Draw the Line?

Most clients believe they know when "enough is enough" in a gaslighting relationship. Unfortunately, though, the trauma bond leads many clients to push past their own boundaries when it comes to abusive and toxic relationships. For example, your client may have told themselves they would leave the relationship if they discovered the gaslighter stealing from them. But after medication, money, and other valuables go missing, they are still in the relationship. Or your client may have told themselves it would be the last straw if the gaslighter hit, shoved, or slapped them. Yet your client denies physical abuse in the relationship even though they tell you that the gaslighter pushed them into a wall "as they were walking by."

The reality is that many clients make several unsuccessful attempts to leave a gaslighting relationship before they do so for good. That's because whenever gaslighters feel their narcissistic supply is dwindling or their partner is at risk of leaving, they will try hoovering the client back into the relationship. If they feel like they are continuing to lose their grip on the client, they may engage in one or more of the following behaviors:

- Threatening to kill themselves if the client leaves
- Saying they have nothing to live for anymore
- Threatening to engage in self-injurious behavior
- Engaging in self-injurious behavior in front of the client (or showing the client what they have done)
- Cleaning firearms in front of the client, particularly if it is done slowly and methodically
- Discussing the amount of ammunition they have in the home
- Telling the client about "bad people" they know
- Telling the client they will never see their children again
- Telling the client they will "get nothing" if they leave and will be "living on the street"
- Threatening to make the client's life a "living hell" if they leave
- Telling the client that it would be "unfortunate" if their pet "accidentally" ran away
- Directly threatening to hurt or kill the client, their children, or their pets

These threats should be taken very seriously, as they can be a precursor to violence. Abuse often follows an escalating cycle, so it's crucial to your client's safety (and that of any children and pets) that they delineate clear boundaries regarding abuse. Encourage your client to state their boundary out loud to you, which forms a social contract that makes it more likely for them to stick to it. You can also consider having your client write down their boundaries and sign and date the document. Remind your client about the power of the trauma bond and that you are mandated to contact social services if their children are subjected to abuse. If your client later reports that this line has been crossed, remind them of the agreement they made with you regarding their limits.

Know Your Limits

Establishing clear boundaries is essential for maintaining healthy and respectful relationships. Here is a list of qualities to consider when defining what you will and will not tolerate in a relationship.

What I Will Accept

1. **Respect and equality:** I expect to be treated with respect, kindness, and equality in all aspects of the relationship. I value open communication, active listening, and the ability to express opinions without fear of judgment or belittlement.

2. **Emotional support:** I require an emotionally supportive, understanding, and empathetic partner. I value a relationship where we can openly share our feelings, provide comfort during difficult times, and support each other's personal growth.

3. **Trust and honesty:** I seek a relationship built on trust and honesty. I expect my partner to be truthful, reliable, and faithful. Open and transparent communication is crucial, and I will work toward fostering trust in the relationship.

4. **Independence and autonomy:** I believe in maintaining my individuality and personal growth within the relationship. I expect my partner to respect my need for independence, personal space, and pursuing my goals and interests.

What I Will Not Tolerate

1. **Abuse and violence:** I will not tolerate physical, emotional, or verbal abuse. Abuse includes acts of violence, intimidation, controlling behaviors, or manipulative tactics. I value my safety and well-being and will not tolerate abusive behavior.

2. **Disrespect and disregard:** I will not tolerate disrespect, humiliation, or dismissive attitudes. I deserve to be treated as an equal and with dignity. I will not accept any behavior undermining my self-worth or belittling my thoughts and opinions.

3. **Dishonesty and betrayal:** I will not tolerate dishonesty, infidelity, or breach of trust. Maintaining honesty and fidelity is essential for building a healthy and trusting relationship.

4. **Lack of communication and ignoring boundaries:** I will not tolerate a partner who consistently dismisses my feelings, refuses to communicate, or disregards my boundaries. I believe in open dialogue, active listening, and respect for each other's boundaries and needs.

I affirm my commitment to self-respect, healthy relationships, and personal growth by acknowledging these boundaries. I understand that it is my responsibility to communicate and reinforce these boundaries with my partner, and I will take appropriate action if they are consistently violated. I recognize that each person's boundaries may vary, and it is essential to regularly reassess and communicate them within the context of the relationship.

Copyright © 2024 Sarkis Media LLC, *A Clinician's Guide to Gaslighting.* All rights reserved.

Elements of a Safety Plan

If your client is living with a gaslighter, they must write out a detailed safety plan that indicates what they will do when the abuse cycle escalates. A thorough safety plan should include the following:

- What items they need to leave home with (e.g., keys, driver's license, phone)
- Who they will take with them (e.g., children, pets)
- How they will exit the home (e.g., front door, window, back door)
- How they will leave the premises (e.g., their car, a ride service, a friend picking them up)
- Where they will go when they leave the home
- Who will hold copies of important papers, extra clothes, extra medication, and another set of car keys in advance of your client leaving the home
- What they will tell their children if they ask about the reasons for leaving home quickly
- Who they will disclose the abuse to and, if the trusted person is a neighbor, also request that this person call 911 if they hear suspicious noises from the home

In addition, the safety plan should include an agreement indicating that your client:

- Acknowledges that this living situation is untenable and is putting their life (and the lives of their children and pets) at risk
- Acknowledges that a gaslighting relationship can quickly escalate into physical abuse at any time
- Understands that they may not be able to exit the home during an abusive episode and may need to deescalate the gaslighter first by giving them what they want
- Will give a copy of this plan to a trusted friend or family member who has no contact with the gaslighter
- Will keep this plan in a safe place and will never give access to the gaslighter

Amend the safety plan as you see fit to reflect the client's living situation, climate, and any other client-specific concerns. Have your client sign and date the safety plan each time you update it. Keep a copy of the plan in their chart or electronic record. If your client feels uncomfortable completing a safety plan, it is essential to discuss the reasons for their hesitation instead of forgoing the idea of a safety plan altogether. Your client may have concerns about the gaslighter finding the plan or may have difficulties coming to terms with the seriousness of the situation. Talk through their fears so you can work together to develop a plan to keep them safe.

Safety Consultants at Domestic Violence Shelters

A client safety consultant is someone who works at a domestic violence shelter and provides expert guidance, support, and resources to survivors of abuse. Clients can utilize a safety consultant whether they are staying at a shelter or still living with a gaslighter. These consultants play a critical role with the following:

- **Risk assessment:** Safety consultants conduct comprehensive assessments to identify and evaluate the safety risks clients face. This includes assessing factors such as the severity of the abuse, history of violence, patterns of control, and the presence of weapons or other high-risk elements. The consultant collaborates with the client to develop a clear understanding of their specific safety concerns.

- **Safety planning:** A consultant works closely with the client to create a personalized safety plan that addresses their unique circumstances and risks. This involves identifying potential triggers for abuse, establishing emergency escape routes, and exploring available support systems. The consultant helps the client develop practical and feasible approaches to minimize risks and increase safety.

- **Resource coordination:** The consultant will assist the client in accessing community resources and services that support their safety and well-being. They may connect them with legal advocacy programs, counseling services, housing assistance, financial support, and health care resources. The consultant is a liaison, helping the client navigate complex systems and facilitating referrals to appropriate professionals.

- **Crisis intervention:** Safety consultants provide immediate support and intervention during crises or high-risk situations. They are trained to respond effectively to emergencies, including violence, stalking, or threats. They work closely with shelter staff and law enforcement to ensure a coordinated response prioritizing client safety and well-being.

- **Education and training:** Consultants conduct safety-related workshops and training sessions for clients and shelter staff. These sessions can empower clients with the knowledge and skills necessary for their safety, including how to recognize the warning signs of escalating violence, establish healthy boundaries, utilize technology safely, and understand legal protections.

- **Collaborative partnerships:** Consultants build and maintain collaborative relationships with community stakeholders, such as law enforcement agencies, legal professionals, and other service providers. They engage in networking and coordination efforts to strengthen the support system available to clients and enhance the overall safety response within the community.

- **Advocacy and empowerment:** Consultants advocate for clients' rights, needs, and safety within the legal and social service systems. They support clients in understanding their legal options, navigating court processes, and accessing appropriate services. This empowers clients to make informed decisions about their safety and helps them reclaim their autonomy and self-determination.

Through all of these efforts, safety consultants play a crucial role in helping clients navigate the challenges of domestic violence, enhance their safety, and rebuild their lives free from abuse.

Create a Safety Plan

Complete the following safety plan to have a course of action when another cycle of abuse begins. Give a copy to your therapist and another to a trusted friend or family member who has no contact with the gaslighter.

1. I will leave my home if any of the following occur (e.g., yelling, gaslighting, hitting):

   _____

2. If I need to leave my home, I will exit in the following way (e.g., door, windows, stairwell):

   _____

3. I will leave the premises via (e.g., my car, ride service, friend):

   _____

4. I will keep my keys, phone, credit card, and driver's license in the following location for ease of access if I need to leave:

   _____

5. I will take the following people and pets with me:

   _____

6. I will leave an extra set of essential documents, clothing, medication, and car keys ahead of time with the following person:

   _____

7. I will say the following to my children if they ask why we are leaving so quickly:

   _____

8. Upon leaving, I will go directly to (e.g., a friend or relative's home, a shelter):

   _____

9. When violence (verbal or physical) escalates, I will move to this area of the house because it has more exits:

   _____

Copyright © 2024 Sarkis Media LLC, *A Clinician's Guide to Gaslighting*. All rights reserved.

10. I can tell the following people about the domestic violence I am experiencing and ask that neighbors call 911 if they hear suspicious noises from my home:

_____

11. I will contact the following advocates for advice on my rights and support (e.g., an attorney, a domestic violence safety consultant, my therapist):

_____

I understand that I may not be able to escape my home and may need to do whatever is possible to protect myself, my children, and my pets, including deescalating my partner by giving them what they want, before I can leave.

_____ Initials

I understand that a relationship with emotional or verbal abuse can escalate to physical abuse at any time.

_____ Initials

I understand that I need to leave this relationship permanently and that my life, and those of my children and pets, are at stake.

_____ Initials

I will keep this plan in a safe place and will give the gaslighter no access to it whatsoever.

_____ Initials

Signature: _____ Date: _____

Copyright © 2024 Sarkis Media LLC, *A Clinician's Guide to Gaslighting*. All rights reserved.

Injunctions and Restraining Orders

When discussing whether it may be in your client's best interest to file an injunction or restraining order, you should carefully assess the circumstances—always prioritizing your client's safety—and strongly recommend that your client meet with a family law attorney. Remember that you cannot give any legal advice as a clinician. Here are some factors for your clients to consider when evaluating the necessity of such legal measures:

- **Imminent danger:** If your client is in immediate physical danger or facing threats of harm, an injunction or restraining order may be crucial to ensure their safety and protection. They should consider any ongoing or escalating threats, stalking behaviors, or incidents of violence that indicate a high risk to their well-being.

- **Pattern of abuse:** Determine whether there exists a pattern of abuse being perpetrated by the individual against whom the injunction or restraining order would be filed. Consider the abuse's severity, frequency, and duration. Make sure to assess for physical, emotional, sexual, psychological, technological, and financial abuse.

- **Fear and emotional distress:** Assess the degree to which the other party's actions are causing your client fear, anxiety, and emotional distress. If your client is experiencing significant emotional and psychological harm, including symptoms of PTSD, due to the relationship, seeking legal protection may be warranted.

- **Power imbalance and control:** Consider the power dynamics within the relationship and whether there is evidence of control, manipulation, or gaslighting. If the client feels trapped, controlled, or unable to assert their autonomy and safety, an injunction or restraining order can provide a legal framework for establishing boundaries and limiting contact.

- **Documentation and evidence:** Ask your client if they have documentation or evidence supporting their abuse claims, such as police reports, medical records, text messages, photos, emails, or witness statements. This information will be requested when your client files for an injunction or restraining order. This evidence can strengthen their case.

- **Client's desire and readiness:** It is essential to respect and support your client's autonomy when helping them decide whether to pursue legal action. Engage in open and nonjudgmental discussions about their options, inform them of the potential benefits and risks, and provide resources to connect them with legal professionals who can offer guidance.

Remember, clinicians are not legal experts, and your client should consult legal professionals to obtain accurate and up-to-date information about the legal processes and requirements in your client's jurisdiction. Collaborate with legal professionals so you are versed in the most current laws and rules that pertain to domestic violence.

When Should You File an Injunction
or Restraining Order?

If someone is purposefully trying to make you feel unsafe, verbally or physically threatening you, stalking you, or calling and texting you incessantly, there are several steps you can take to protect your well-being. First, block the gaslighter on your phone, email, and social media accounts. Tell a trusted friend or family member to keep an eye on the gaslighter's social media accounts and to screenshot and report any threats to you immediately.

Second, consult with a family law attorney about whether you may meet the criteria for an injunction or restraining order. You can file these orders against anyone harassing, stalking, or abusing you, whether that person is a spouse, partner, parent, sibling, friend, coworker, employer, or employee. An attorney can tell you about the different injunctions or restraining orders and how to apply for one. The gaslighter may not contact or be near your home or workplace if a judge grants you one. The protection may also be extended to your children as well.

If the gaslighter is engaging in any of the following behaviors, it may necessitate an injunction or restraining order:

- Holding you against your will

- Harassment

- Verbal threats (including to your children, pets, or family members)

- Stalking

- Physical abuse

- Sexual assault

- Threatening you with firearms or other weapons

- Breaking into your home or workplace

- Trespassing on your property

- Abusing your children or pets

You may need to take pictures of any injury to you, or damage to your belongings and home, and attach them to the request. Be aware that a judge may not grant an injunction or restraining order without sufficient information, so record in as much detail as possible what you have experienced, including dates, times, direct quotes, and names of witnesses. Talk with your therapist about what to disclose for an injunction or restraining order. They may also remember details you have disclosed to them that you may not have thought of since the abusive episode.

When the Client Is Coparenting with a Gaslighter

Although leaving a gaslighting relationship is difficult enough, the situation can become even more tenuous when children are involved. Coparenting with a gaslighter is a high-conflict parenting situation, as the gaslighter will often attempt to control and punish the other parent through their children. For example, they might use the children as pawns to leverage the other parent or engage in a smear campaign against them. Your client may have a gaslighting coparent if the other parent:

- "Accidentally" leaves divorce or custody documents out for their children to see

- Makes comments to the children about how your client has "taken all of my money"

- Uses the court system to bankrupt your client

- Tells the children to call the gaslighter's new partner "Mom" or "Dad"

- Makes the children call your client by their first name instead of "Mom" or "Dad"

- Changes the pickup schedule with little notice

- Has someone else take care of the children and doesn't honor the right of first refusal

- Refuses to pay child support or reimburse for agreed-upon expenses

- Refuses to exchange the children at the agreed-upon time and location

- Spreads rumors about your client being an unfit parent

- Threatens to take the children away

- Calls in false abuse reports

- Refuses to have the children seek care from a mental health professional

- Refuses to give the children their prescribed medication

- Separates the children into different roles (e.g., a golden child and a scapegoat)

- Listens in on phone calls between your client and their child

- Interferes with or gatekeeps access to the children (e.g., planning a fun trip during your client's time with the children)

If the gaslighting coparent has significant access to wealth, they may use the court system to abuse the other parent by engaging in multiple filings of motions, depositions, and trials. Some clients have even had to file bankruptcy or represent themselves (known as "pro se") because of the significant court costs they have incurred due to the gaslighter. All of these behaviors are considered a form of parental alienation, meaning that they are designed to drive a wedge between the non-gaslighting parent and their children. While coparenting with a gaslighter is a long-term and likely emotionally draining process, there are steps your client can take to protect themselves and their children.

Recommendations for Effective Coparenting

If your client is coparenting with a gaslighter, recommend they meet with a family law attorney to learn their rights and their children's rights. If your client cannot afford an attorney, many family law attorneys offer their services pro bono or at a sliding fee scale. Be aware that many gaslighters will tell the coparent that it will be "easier" if they don't use attorneys. It will not be easier—your client's rights are at stake.

Your client will also need a detailed parenting plan, which serves as a fallback when a high-conflict parent is causing difficulties. Your client can point to the parenting plan as the default or deciding factor in disputes. A thorough parenting plan should include specific details on the following:

- Points of exchange (e.g., school, curbside, neutral location)
- Who will exchange the children
- How long the coparent has to wait at the exchange point before time-sharing reverts to them
- Who is and isn't allowed to be with the children
- Right of first refusal
- Holiday schedules
- Notification time required for trips out of the state and out of the country
- Who has final decision-making ability in various areas
- School and after-school care decisions
- Who is responsible for what costs (including school or car costs)
- Who will attend what school, sports, or other events

The parenting plan should also include a statement indicating that the plan will be revisited when the children start school (if they are not yet attending) or enter middle or high school. Encourage your client to speak to their attorney for more information on what should be included in a parenting plan when there is a high-conflict coparent. If your client is concerned or confused about their attorney's recommendations, encourage them to write down these concerns and address them with their attorney. Be clear with your client that you are not an attorney and can't give legal advice.

Finally, encourage your client to consider working with a parent coordinator, who is appointed by the court to help parents communicate effectively and work in the best interests of their children. Parent coordinators are usually mental health professionals or attorneys. Some states have required certification processes for becoming a parent coordinator. These individuals will usually meet with each parent alone and then have meetings with both parents present. Items to be discussed include:

- School placement decisions
- Expense distribution

- Medical care

- Mental health counseling

- Sports and other activities

- Contact with each parent's new partner

- Exchange of children

- Trips with children

- Time-sharing and custody

- Changes to the schedule

Both parents must participate equally for a parent coordinator to be most effective. While your client can't control their coparent's behavior, they have control over their own actions and attitudes.

Use a Coparenting App

You might find it extremely difficult to communicate with a gaslighting coparent via text, email, or phone. Every interaction might seem like it results in you being shamed or the gaslighter telling you that you are a terrible parent, a terrible person, or worse. They may frequently steer the conversation off-topic and personally attack you. To decrease these interactions, consider using a coparenting app as your main point of communication with your coparent.

The following are the benefits of using a coparenting app:

- There is a date and time stamp for all communication.

- It provides a shared calendar for your children's appointments, games, and other activities.

- You have one location for submitting receipts for reimbursement of expenses.

- It includes a "tone detector" that notifies you when you are using language that may be inappropriate.

- It allows you to document all communications, including inappropriate and abusive statements by your coparent.

- You can easily print out PDFs of your conversations to give to your attorney.

- It decreases the coparent's ability to claim you gave them false information.

Consider using a coparenting app and adding it to your parenting plan if you are coparenting with someone who continually twists your words, verbally abuses you, or gaslights you. Protect yourself and your kids by having one stop for documentation, scheduling, and reimbursement.

Tips on Coparenting with a Gaslighter

Coparenting with a gaslighter can be an emotionally draining experience. You can follow these tips to help reduce your burden:

- Communicate only through a coparenting app (and include this app in your parenting plan).

- Use the gray rock method when interacting with the coparent.

- Be clear and firm with the time-sharing or custody schedule.

- Seek counsel from your attorney when needed.

- Never speak badly about your children's other parent.

- Answer your children's questions about their parent as kindly as possible.

- Ask general questions about what your children did with the other parent during their time without asking for details.

- Wait at least six months into a committed relationship before introducing your children to a new partner.

- Be aware that anything you say to your children could be transmitted to the coparent.

- Use a detailed parenting plan as the default if there is a dispute.

- Consider whether the issue is something worth arguing about.

- Consider your children's well-being first.

- Speak directly to your coparent through the app instead of sending messages through your children.

- Consider a parallel parenting style.

Copyright © 2024 Sarkis Media LLC, *A Clinician's Guide to Gaslighting*. All rights reserved.

Parallel Parenting

A parallel parenting style may work best when coparenting with a gaslighter or otherwise abusive person. It can be less stressful and allow fewer opportunities for abuse from your coparent. In this style of coparenting:

- Parenting is done completely independently.

- Each home has its own guidelines and parenting style.

- Communication is only done via a coparenting app.

- Parents only communicate in emergencies.

- Parents have separate meetings with teachers, or one parent calls the teacher later for an update.

- One parent attends the child's doctor appointments, and the other contacts the doctor for a summary.

- Each parent has their own items for their children so things are not carried back and forth.

- Parents don't attend the same events or games.

- The children have their own phones, so you don't need to call the other parent.

- There is a detailed parenting plan stating specific exchange times and locations, dates of time-sharing and custody, and in what areas each parent has decision-making power.

Ask your family law attorney if parallel parenting may be recommended. Ensure your attorney knows about the history of emotional abuse in your relationship.

Copyright © 2024 Sarkis Media LLC, *A Clinician's Guide to Gaslighting*. All rights reserved.

What to Ask a Family Law Attorney During a Consultation

When you meet with a family law attorney, you may feel intimidated and even ashamed. Both these feelings are normal. You are meeting with an expert and sharing your story, much of which you have likely never shared with anyone else. To help you through your first meeting, consider asking the following questions:

- What experience do you have with clients with high-conflict, gaslighting, or narcissistic coparents?

- At what point would you recommend going to court rather than mediation?

- How much is the retainer, and what does it cover?

- What's your policy on returning phone calls or emails?

- Will I be working with you or an associate?

- Do you meet with clients to review a case before going to mediation or trial?

- What's the best way to relay new information to you? Phone, email, text, or portal?

- What constitutes an emergency in coparenting?

- What should I do if I feel my children's safety is jeopardized?

- How far am I legally allowed to move away from the coparent?

- What are your recommendations for time-sharing or custody with a high-conflict coparent?

- Do you know or have you worked with my coparent's attorney before?

- What's the best thing I can do now to protect my and my children's rights?

- Who do you recommend leaves the marital home?

- Is collaborative divorce an option in this case?

- Do you recommend a parent coordinator? Whom do you recommend?

186   Copyright © 2024 Sarkis Media LLC, *A Clinician's Guide to Gaslighting.* All rights reserved.

Develop a Parenting Plan

Use this worksheet when meeting with your attorney to briefly explain what you think is in the best interest of you and your children. Know that only in rare cases will a judge deny custody to your coparent.

Names of children and dates of birth:

_____

_____

Preferred time-sharing or custody (circle all that apply):

      Every other weekend and one weekday   One week on, one week off

      Sunday through Wednesday   Thursday through Saturday

      Other: _____

Proposed exchange time and location:

_____

How children will be exchanged (circle all that apply):

      Curbside   At school   At relative's home: _____

I am okay with the following people watching my children:

_____

_____

I do not want the following people to watch my children:

_____

_____

I will wait _____ (amount of time) at an exchange point without communication from my coparent before time-sharing or custody reverts to me.

Copyright © 2024 Sarkis Media LLC, *A Clinician's Guide to Gaslighting.* All rights reserved.

If I or my coparent will be away from our children for _____ (amount of time) or longer during my time-sharing or custody, I will contact my coparent to give them the right of first refusal.

If I plan to take an out-of-state trip with our children, I will notify my coparent _____ (amount of time) ahead of the trip and will give them an itinerary.

If I plan to take a trip out of the country with our children, I will notify my coparent _____ (amount of time) ahead of the trip and will give them an itinerary.

When my coparent has time-sharing or custody, I will contact my children for a 30-minute phone call at _____ (time).

In the following areas, I am okay with the final decisions being made by (circle preference):

Medical:	Me	Coparent	Both
After-school activities:	Me	Coparent	Both
Counseling:	Me	Coparent	Both
Sports activities:	Me	Coparent	Both
School trips:	Me	Coparent	Both
School selection:	Me	Coparent	Both
Orthodontics:	Me	Coparent	Both
Summer activities:	Me	Coparent	Both
School supplies/clothing:	Me	Coparent	Both
Tutoring:	Me	Coparent	Both

If both of us die, I would like guardianship of our children to go to:

_____

College or trade school expenses for our children should be paid as follows (circle one):

Equally   Myself   Coparent   Our children will fund this themselves

A car for our children should be paid as follows (circle one):

Equally   Myself   Coparent   We will not be purchasing a car

Copyright © 2024 Sarkis Media LLC, *A Clinician's Guide to Gaslighting*. All rights reserved.

CHAPTER 12

Rebuilding

Leaving a relationship where abuse has occurred can be traumatic, and it can take time for a client to rebuild a sense of self and reach a new normal. There are several reasons why this process can be challenging and harrowing. First, there is the issue of recognizing and overcoming the trauma bond. Given that the trauma bond has an intense hold over its victims, many clients have trouble remembering themselves as individuals with their own wants, needs, and opinions. Then there is the importance of maintaining no-contact or low-contact. The gaslighter will typically attempt intense hoovering behaviors after the client has left the relationship, making it difficult for them to move on.

In this chapter, you will learn how to help your client rebuild after leaving a gaslighting relationship, which includes reestablishing contact with supportive friends and family members from whom the client was estranged and volunteering in the community to reconnect them with their passions and help them work toward a common goal. You will also explore how to best support clients who seek closure and forgiveness, especially given that this is unlikely to occur on behalf of the gaslighter. For many clients, writing an unsent letter to the gaslighter can help heal these wounds.

Areas of Focus in Therapy When Rebuilding

When working with a client who has left a gaslighting relationship, it is essential to consider whether their basic wants and needs are being met before you delve deeper into family of origin issues and trauma. Consider whether your client:

- Has a stable and safe place to live

- Is maintaining no-contact or low-contact with the gaslighter

- Has their children and pets safely with them

- Has enrolled their children in school

- Has income or money saved for expenditures

- Is not experiencing episodes of dissociation that interfere with daily functioning

- Has processed their grief over the loss of the relationship

- Has access to legal services

- Is following the advice of their attorney

- Has created a temporary coparenting plan with their attorney

- Has access to the marital home

- Is being supported by understanding family or friends

- Has a restraining order or injunction in place if needed

As illustrated by Maslow's hierarchy of needs, your client must fulfill their most basic needs—the foundational levels of the pyramid—before they can successfully focus on other areas in therapy that are part of the higher levels of the pyramid.

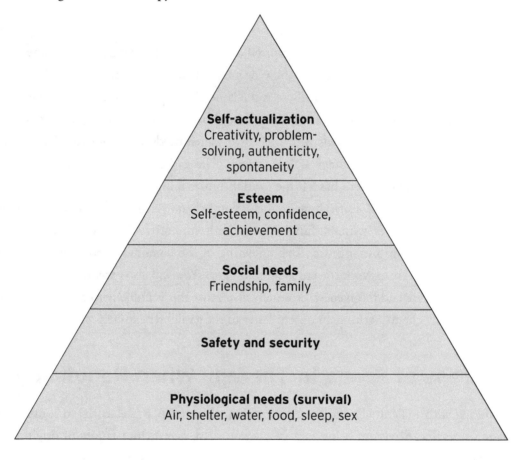

Self-actualization
Creativity, problem-solving, authenticity, spontaneity

Esteem
Self-esteem, confidence, achievement

Social needs
Friendship, family

Safety and security

Physiological needs (survival)
Air, shelter, water, food, sleep, sex

If your client does not have their lower-level needs met, there are several actionable steps you can take to help them. For example, if your client lacks safe housing, you can assist them in accessing local resources such as shelters, housing assistance programs, or community organizations that provide temporary or permanent housing solutions. You can also help them navigate the social service system by accompanying them to appointments, assisting with paperwork, or advocating on their behalf to secure safe housing. Or if your client is having difficulty accessing legal services, you can connect them with local legal aid organizations that provide low-cost or pro bono legal services and help them gather necessary documents to prepare for their appointment. You can also collaborate with multidisciplinary teams, such as social workers, housing agencies, legal professionals, or community organizations, to provide comprehensive support as needed. Regardless, you should regularly assess your client's safety and well-being and make necessary referrals to ensure their immediate needs are addressed alongside their therapeutic journey.

Client Worksheet

Checklist for Rebuilding

After you have ended a relationship with a gaslighter, it can be helpful to know what you might need to do during this time to rebuild a safe, healthy, and fulfilling life. Review the following list and see how many of these items you have completed:

- ❏ I have a safe, affordable place to live.

- ❏ My children are safe and enrolled in school.

- ❏ I have a coparenting plan in place.

- ❏ I have a source of income or savings.

- ❏ I have structure to my day.

- ❏ I eat regularly.

- ❏ I get enough sleep each night.

- ❏ I have a reliable form of transportation.

- ❏ I have my own health insurance or can find access to affordable health care without insurance.

- ❏ I have received a checkup from a primary care provider in the past year.

- ❏ I have received a checkup from a dentist in the past year.

- ❏ My recommended preventive care is up to date (e.g., mammogram, pap smear, colonoscopy, immunizations).

- ❏ I have an attorney if needed.

- ❏ I have a bank account in my name only.

- ❏ I make time every day to take care of myself.

- ❏ I make time for fun.

- ❏ I have a support network of trustworthy friends and family members.

The more items you've checked off, the further you are progressing toward rebuilding. Try to make progress toward any unchecked items. Progress still counts, even if it feels like you are making small changes. Small changes add up quickly.

Copyright © 2024 Sarkis Media LLC, *A Clinician's Guide to Gaslighting*. All rights reserved.

The Importance of Maintaining
No-Contact or Low-Contact

You may find that once you have left the gaslighter, they pull out all the stops to try to hoover you back into contact with them. They may promise you that things will be better—that they will change—and they may threaten you when sweet-talking you isn't working. When this happens, it's important to notice what you probably won't hear from the gaslighter: a full apology where they take responsibility for their behavior *without blaming you*. If you find yourself believing that the gaslighter is serious about making things work this time, see if they meet any of the following criteria:

❒ They have apologized without being asked to apologize.

❒ They have made full amends to you (e.g., repaid debts and replaced items they broke).

❒ They have apologized and made amends to any family and friends they have lied to.

❒ They have taken full responsibility for their behavior.

❒ They have not attempted to shift blame to you when apologizing.

❒ They have addressed how they are working to change their behavior.

❒ They have started therapy and are attending it every week.

❒ They have shown consistent changes in their behavior over at least six months.

❒ They have been able to express their feelings and own them.

❒ They are receiving medication and taking it as prescribed for any medical conditions.

If the gaslighter has not met all of these criteria, seriously consider continuing no-contact or low-contact. At the bare minimum, a gaslighter who is in recovery will be able to admit that their behavior was abusive and regularly attend intensive individual therapy. Anything less will most likely result in the gaslighter reverting to their old behaviors.

Copyright © 2024 Sarkis Media LLC, *A Clinician's Guide to Gaslighting*. All rights reserved.

Helping Your Client Make New Connections and Reestablish Healthy Connections

It can be difficult for your client to rebuild bonds with loved ones after estrangement, particularly when gaslighting or trauma has strained the relationship. It is understandable that your client's family and friends may have apprehensions or reservations about reconnecting. To increase the chances of repairing the relationship, it is essential that your client allow the other person to set the pace for connection. Encourage your client to demonstrate patience, understanding, and respect throughout this process, remembering that rebuilding trust takes time and consistency. The most effective way your client can demonstrate their commitment to reestablishing the relationship is through their actions—by consistently showing up, keeping promises, and respecting boundaries. These behaviors allow loved ones to witness the client's growth and gradually rebuild trust. Your client should also take accountability for anything they did that may have contributed to the estrangement.

When it comes to making new friends, encourage your client to seek out activities with groups of like-minded individuals who share similar interests and values. For example, if your client enjoys reading, they might join a local book club or sign up for events hosted at the local library. Or if your client is into fitness, encourage them to join a sports league or seek out exercise classes at the YMCA. Remind clients that building new friendships takes time and effort. Encourage them to be patient and realistic about the process, understanding that not every connection will develop into a deep friendship. Some clients may also benefit from social skills and assertiveness training to help them develop the confidence to engage in social situations and initiate conversations. Role-playing scenarios or practicing social interactions in therapy can enhance their skills and reduce anxiety, especially after their confidence has been eroded in the gaslighting relationship.

**Client
Worksheet**

Bull's-Eye: People You Know

Being in a relationship with a gaslighter can leave you feeling extremely isolated. You may have distanced yourself from friends and family because the gaslighter told you these people were a bad influence or were talking about you behind your back. Either way, these were most likely lies that the gaslighter told to estrange you from the people who had your best interests at heart. Right now, you may be feeling like you don't have much support. Here's a visual exercise to help you understand how many people care about you.

In the center of the bull's-eye, write the names of people you can call at any time of the day or night if you need something. This may include lifelong friends, best friends, and close family members. In the next ring, write the names of people you can call during the day if you need something. Examples include your neighbors, doctors, and good friends from work. In the outer ring, write down acquaintances you know from other activities, like people you might know from your children's school or your house of worship. These may be kind people that you might like to get to know better.

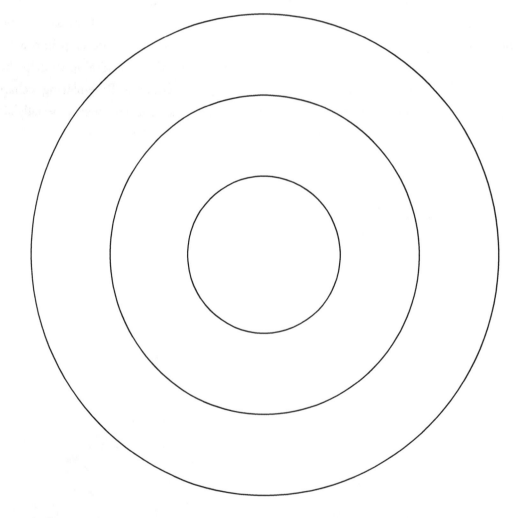

Copyright © 2024 Sarkis Media LLC, *A Clinician's Guide to Gaslighting*. All rights reserved.

After filling out the bull's-eye, what have you learned about your support network?

_____

_____

_____

_____

Would you like to expand your support network? Why or why not?

_____

_____

_____

_____

If you feel your support network is too small, what are some ways you could meet new people?

_____

_____

_____

_____

Who are some people in your support network that you could get to know better?

_____

_____

_____

_____

Reconnecting with Trusted Family and Friends

Part of healing from gaslighting is reconnecting with supportive family and friends from whom you have been isolated. You are not obligated to share your story when reconnecting with a loved one, even if they ask what happened. It is entirely up to you whether or not you discuss your experience. If you do share your story, ensure it is with someone trustworthy who will keep your disclosure confidential. If you doubt whether you can trust someone, consider holding off on sharing your story and talk it over with your therapist first.

If you feel uncomfortable reconnecting with family and friends, know that it's normal to feel this way. Here are some things you can say to make things a little easier:

- "We haven't spoken in a while, but I'd like to reconnect with you."

- "I'd love to get together and catch up."

- "This is kind of awkward, but I've missed you and want to talk."

You may find that your friends and family are so excited to hear from you that you can't even get a sentence out before they tell you how much they've missed you and want to get together soon. However, it may be that someone you contact isn't interested in reconnecting. It can be difficult to experience that kind of rejection. But if that's the case, know that the decision is about them and not you. Sometimes it just takes time to build up a relationship again. If you decide this is a relationship you truly want to rebuild, talk about it with that person and give them time, but always remember to respect the other person's boundaries and decisions regarding the relationship.

Copyright © 2024 Sarkis Media LLC, *A Clinician's Guide to Gaslighting*. All rights reserved.

Volunteering

Volunteering can be essential to your client's healing and rebuilding plan. Not only can volunteering give your client a sense of mission and purpose during this challenging life transition, but it can also:

- Reintroduce your client to the community

- Connect your client with others who have a common interest

- Provide your client with structure during a time of upheaval

- Provide your client with an opportunity for possible employment in the organization

- Improve your client's quality of life

- Allow your client to practice social skills in a safe environment

There are endless types of organizations that your client can contact for volunteer opportunities, depending on their interests, schedule, and level of availability. When proposing volunteer organization options to your client, it's important to consider opportunities that align with their skills and therapeutic goals. Volunteering should be a positive and fulfilling experience, so you want your client to choose opportunities that resonate with them. Here are some common volunteer organization options you may want to suggest:

- **Crisis hotlines:** Many crisis hotlines and helplines need volunteers to provide emotional support, crisis intervention, and resource referrals to distressed individuals. Only consider this option for clients who have done extensive work on their trauma, as it may trigger them.

- **Homeless shelters and transitional housing programs:** Volunteering at shelters or transitional housing programs can allow clients to engage in direct service, providing support and resources to individuals experiencing homelessness. This experience can deepen clients' understanding of diverse experiences and foster empathy.

- **School-based mentoring programs:** Many schools have mentoring programs where volunteers can support students with their schoolwork, career plans, athletics, skill development, and more.

- **Arts programs:** Community art centers and museums may need guides, ushers, and mentors to help install exhibits, plan special events, assist visitors, provide guided tours, and more.

- **Animal-assisted therapy programs:** Animal shelters and animal-assisted therapy programs often welcome volunteers.

- **LGBTQIA+ support organizations:** Clients passionate about LGBTQIA+ rights may find it fulfilling to volunteer with local or national organizations that provide support, education, and resources to the LGBTQIA+ community.

No matter the type of volunteer work your client gravitates to, it is essential for them to thoroughly research the organization they would like to work with. Because your client may be particularly vulnerable to gaslighting during this fragile time, they must search for reputable organizations that do not exploit their members. Some potential warning signs of unethical organizations include those that contact volunteers at all hours, mismanage organization funds, sign up volunteers without asking for their permission, change the time and location of volunteer events without notice, pressure volunteers to do questionable activities, and dismiss volunteers on a whim and then ask them back. Encourage your clients to discuss their potential opportunities with you.

Finding a Healthy Volunteering Opportunity

Volunteering has been shown to improve mental and physical health, which is crucial during a life change. When you're looking into different organizations that you might want to volunteer your time to, look for the following characteristics, which are all indicators of reputable and ethical organizations:

- You can give as little or as much time as you'd like.

- There is a supervisor or someone to go to if you have questions.

- Most of the organization's funds go directly to those they intend to help.

- You can change your mind about volunteering, which is entirely okay with the organization.

- There are structured times to volunteer, which are stable and predictable.

- Your time away from the organization is respected, and you aren't pressured to spend more time volunteering.

- You aren't pressured to invest your own money in the organization.

You can use local, state, or federal websites to help you explore different volunteer opportunities in your area and match your interests with an organization that is right for you.

Copyright © 2024 Sarkis Media LLC, *A Clinician's Guide to Gaslighting*. All rights reserved.

The Question of Dating

Many clients wonder when it is appropriate to start dating after ending a romantic relationship with a gaslighter. The correct answer is "There is no timeline." Everyone heals at a different pace, and you must honor and respect your client's journey toward healing and recovery. The effects of gaslighting can be profound and complex, and rushing into a new relationship can potentially lead to repeating harmful patterns or retraumatization.

While every individual's healing journey is unique, clients should hold off on dating if they still struggle with trust issues or have unresolved feelings toward the gaslighter. They may also need more time if they have a strong need for external validation and are seeking a new relationship to fill a void or regain self-esteem. When a client is focused more on finding someone to rescue or "fix" them—rather than building a healthy and equal partnership—they need to spend more time introspecting and developing a sense of self before entering the dating process. Encourage your client to prioritize self-care and focus on their healing process before they pursue new relationships.

On the other hand, your client may be ready to start dating if they have developed healthy coping mechanisms to manage triggers, established a strong sense of self, and learned how to assert themselves and set boundaries in relationships. Here are some additional signs that your client may be ready to start dating:

- They have moved past being unable to consider an intimate relationship with anyone other than their former partner.

- They understand that a healthy partner adds to the happiness they achieve when they are single.

- They know what constitutes a healthy relationship.

- They feel more confident about meeting new people.

- They no longer ruminate about their former partner.

- They have reconnected with emotionally healthy family and friends.

- They have moved toward a secure attachment style.

- They consider the ending of a relationship as a natural part of life instead of a devastating event.

You can also encourage your client to write down what they want in a partner, including any physical, emotional, and spiritual attributes. If your client meets someone that they are interested in, encourage them to look at the list they created. It can help add logical and practical thinking to an emotionally charged process.

Finally, if your client looks into online dating as a way to find a potential match, know that gaslighters, sociopaths, and narcissists may seek vulnerabilities in online dating profiles to lure in potential victims, putting your client at greater risk of sexual assault and violence (Pooley & Boxall, 2020; Valentine et al., 2022). For those reasons, encourage your clients to meet new people by joining a common interest group, such as a book club, sports team, alumni organization, hiking group, crafting group, travel club, or language-learning class. While your client may not meet a potential mate in the group, they can still build friendships based on common interests.

Signs of a Gaslighter on a First Date

Going on a first date can be overwhelming, even more so when you're meeting up with someone you've only interacted with online. If your date engages in any of the behaviors below, consider leaving the date early, as these are all signs of gaslighting. Don't worry about looking rude; every second spent with a gaslighter makes you more likely to be sucked into their scheme. Excuse yourself and leave.

- They don't look like their online profile.

- The "facts" they give you in person don't match what you were told on the dating app, via text messages, or on the phone.

- They talk mostly about themselves and don't ask about you.

- They ask you deeply personal questions, including about any past trauma.

- They "trauma dump" or tell you too much personal information too quickly.

- They arrive late with no apology or explanation.

- They are demeaning or otherwise rude to waitstaff or other service providers.

- They show irritation or anger when you decline to share personal information with them.

- They tell you that you are the "best," "the most beautiful," or "perfect."

- They speak about family members or exes in derogatory terms.

- They often speak about their exes or are very focused on one ex.

- They talk about commitment with you, including moving in together.

- They ask you about your vulnerabilities.

- They blame others for their issues.

- They play the "victim role" in their life.

- You feel emotionally drained after being with them for a short time.

If you sense any red flags or something seems off during the date, review this with your therapist.

Copyright © 2024 Sarkis Media LLC, *A Clinician's Guide to Gaslighting*. All rights reserved.

Complicated Grief

Complicated grief, also known as prolonged grief disorder, is a persistent and intense form of grief that extends beyond the expected mourning period and significantly impairs an individual's functioning. Complicated grief can manifest in various ways, including feelings of disbelief, bitterness, anger, difficulty accepting the loss, and a sense of meaninglessness. Among victims of gaslighting, complicated grief can often emerge due to the unique dynamics of the abusive relationship. When the relationship ends, whether through separation, escape, or intervention, the loss experienced can be layered with complex emotions, including grief for the loss of the relationship itself and grief for the loss of the client's sense of self, trust, and emotional well-being.

Working through complicated grief requires time, patience, and support. As a clinician, you must provide a safe and nonjudgmental space for your client to grieve and mourn, allowing them to process their emotions and ultimately find a path toward acceptance and growth. You may have to use certain cognitive-behavioral techniques to challenge and reframe distorted beliefs that your client has as a result of gaslighting, such as the belief that they are unworthy of finding happiness or that they are at fault for the way the relationship played out. This process allows the client to develop a more adaptive perspective that reduces feelings of shame. You should also incorporate trauma-focused interventions to address any trauma symptoms and support the client in processing their traumatic experiences. Additionally, you might incorporate other evidence-based modalities, such as mindfulness, solution-focused therapy, narrative therapy, or interpersonal therapy, depending on the client's specific needs and goals.

Complicated Grief

The decision to go no-contact or low-contact with a gaslighter is never made lightly. It took quite a bit of thought and sadness to come to terms with the fact that this person did not have your best interests in mind and that it was best for you to disconnect from them. Whenever you lose a relationship, whether it is through death, divorce, or separation, you experience grief. However, when the relationship has been a particularly difficult one, and one where you experienced a trauma bond, you may feel what is called *complicated grief.*

Complicated grief is a more intense level of sorrow than "standard" grief. This type of grief may seem never-ending, like you are stuck in your grief. The pain may persist for months or even years. If you have previously been diagnosed with posttraumatic stress disorder (PTSD), you may be more likely to experience complicated grief after ending a relationship with a gaslighter.

Signs of complicated grief include:

- Intense, unbearable yearning or emotional pain that never seems to go away

- Thoughts of the person that seem to take over your brain and are difficult to stop

- Difficulties picturing a future without this person

- Isolating yourself from people

- Intense feelings of guilt

- Desire to disappear or go to sleep and not wake up

- Uncontrollable anger

- Inability to look forward to anything

- Feeling that your life has no meaning

- Difficulty holding a job or completing daily tasks

If you are experiencing any of these symptoms, or your grief has continued for six months or more, talk to your therapist about the possibility of having complicated grief.

Helping Your Client Get Closure

Victims of gaslighting often want closure as they rebuild their sense of self and move forward in life. For many clients, this means they want the gaslighter to take ownership of their behaviors or, at the very least, offer an explanation. However, the reality is that most clients will never get closure from a gaslighter. Gaslighters rarely offer genuine apologies, and many never entirely leave a client's life, especially when children are involved, which can leave clients feeling stuck and resentful.

The concept of closure in the context of therapeutic healing can be differentiated into two perspectives: the external closure clients often seek, such as an apology or acknowledgment of wrongdoing from the gaslighter, versus the more realistic and achievable form of closure that focuses on accepting and coming to terms with what happened. Although clients often believe that obtaining closure from the gaslighter will bring them inner peace and healing, relying solely on external factors for closure can be challenging and unpredictable. In most cases, the gaslighter will not take responsibility or provide the desired outcome, which can leave the client feeling stuck and unable to move forward.

Clients don't necessarily need answers to move on from a gaslighter. Understanding the "why" behind a gaslighter's manipulation and abuse will not lessen your client's pain. Although you likely can't help your client get closure in the form of an apology or explanation, you can help them come to terms with the past so they can let go and move forward. If your client is interested in getting closure, consider recommending the following activities:

- Writing an unsent letter to the gaslighter
- Having a private ceremony or ritual to say goodbye to the person and relationship
- Writing or dictating an essay or book
- Creating artwork about their experience
- Doing a guided visualization where your client says goodbye to the gaslighter and discovers what they have learned from the experience

These activities empower clients to let go of their emotional burden, make meaning out of their experiences, and find peace and resolution within themselves. As they release themselves from the grip of the past, they can cultivate resilience and embrace a future where they can grow, heal, and thrive. Ultimately, this closure allows clients to reclaim their power and create a new narrative.

Importantly, these activities don't require your client to forgive their abuser or condone their abusive treatment in any way. Forgiving the other person is not a prerequisite to healing and can potentially do more harm. However, it may be necessary for your client to practice forgiving *themselves*, primarily if they blame themselves for the gaslighter's behavior. Common statements you may hear from clients who would benefit from self-forgiveness include:

- "I made my bed; now I need to lie in it."
- "I can't believe I was that naive."
- "This is all my fault."

- "Maybe they were right—that I am crazy."

- "I deserve every bad thing that happens to me."

Clients in this situation may be angry that they didn't notice signs of gaslighting earlier in their relationship. Some may also use self-blame as a way to avoid feeling anger toward the gaslighter. To help them move forward, you will want to emphasize that gaslighting can be very difficult to detect because the abuser lures their victims in with love bombing and cranks up the abuse slowly. People can be in gaslighting relationships for decades without realizing it. You also want to mention that the very purpose of a gaslighter's abusive behavior is to make their victims feel like they are the ones to blame for the dysfunction. Gaslighters tirelessly make their victims feel like perpetrators (see the discussion of DARVO in chapter 1).

To facilitate closure and self-forgiveness, help your client focus on what they have learned from this experience. For example, since ending the gaslighting relationship, your client may feel:

- A greater understanding of themselves

- Support from loved ones that they didn't expect

- More resilient and better able to face life's difficulties

Finally, time helps with closure, but only if your client can keep no-contact or low-contact with the gaslighter. Otherwise, your client is continually opening the wound. If your client has difficulty maintaining no-contact or low-contact, discuss what makes it so challenging, including the trauma bond (see chapter 6).

Writing an Unsent Letter

Writing a letter to someone who hurt you, even if you don't (or can't) send that letter, can help you work through your trauma and find a sense of resolution in your healing. Write as much as you want, and let your words flow freely. Continue to write without criticizing or stopping yourself. If you prefer not to write, dictating a letter works just as well. Let the gaslighter know how they made you feel, how they impacted you, and what you learned from the experience.

Copyright © 2024 Sarkis Media LLC, *A Clinician's Guide to Gaslighting*. All rights reserved.

CHAPTER 13

Vicarious Trauma and Compassion Fatigue

Working with clients who have experienced gaslighting and other forms of emotional abuse can increase your chances of developing vicarious trauma, in which you internalize your client's suffering and experience it as your own. It may also activate your own history of trauma, making it more challenging to effectively work with clients. In this chapter, you will learn about vicarious trauma, including why it happens and what makes you vulnerable. You will also explore a byproduct of vicarious trauma—burnout—and understand the importance of practicing good self-care, having supportive supervision, seeking therapy, having strong peer support, and maintaining balanced and diverse caseloads to stay in balance.

Are You Experiencing Vicarious Trauma?

It is common for individuals in helping professions to experience vicarious trauma as a function of their work. Vicarious trauma, also known as secondary trauma, refers to the emotional and psychological impact of repeatedly hearing about and engaging with another person's suffering. In the therapeutic context, it occurs when a clinician is exposed to their clients' suffering and, over time, absorbs their pain. While maintaining professional boundaries is crucial, some clinicians find it challenging to emotionally detach themselves from their clients' experiences. They may personally identify with clients' struggles or carry the weight of their clients' pain. Clinicians may also have unresolved traumas that get reactivated when working with clients with similar experiences.

Vicarious trauma shares similarities with compassion fatigue, a state of emotional exhaustion and reduced empathy resulting from providing care and support to others. Compassion fatigue can arise from the cumulative exposure to your clients' trauma and the emotional demands of the therapeutic work, leading to a depletion of your emotional resources and a sense of overwhelm. Both vicarious trauma and compassion fatigue highlight the toll that empathetically engaging with clients can have on clinicians.

You may be experiencing vicarious trauma if you are:

- Having increased flashbacks to your trauma

- Having nightmares about your client's trauma

- Treating people poorly in your personal life because they remind you of your client's abuser

- Becoming overly emotionally attached to your client
- Trying to "fix" your client's issues rather than supporting and guiding them
- Feeling like you aren't making a difference at work or in your personal life
- Viewing the world in a more cynical or pessimistic way
- Engaging in self-injurious behaviors
- Relapsing into addictive behaviors as a way to cope
- Experiencing an increase in somatic symptoms (e.g., headaches, stomachaches)
- Experiencing bouts of anger that you cannot resolve

If you are experiencing any of these symptoms, you must seek counseling. Not only will these symptoms interfere with your ability to serve as an effective resource for your clients, but they will also increase the likelihood that you will experience burnout and leave the profession altogether.

Burnout

Burnout is a state of physical, emotional, and mental exhaustion that results from chronic work-related stress. Burnout is not specific to trauma exposure but can result from various factors, such as overwhelming workloads, lack of resources, or a perceived imbalance between your job demands and available coping strategies. It is characterized by three main dimensions:

- **Emotional exhaustion** is a feeling of being drained and depleted of emotional resources. Emotional exhaustion can contribute to emotional detachment or numbness, where clinicians distance themselves from their clients' emotional experiences as a self-protective mechanism. They may create this distance to prevent themselves from becoming overwhelmed by the emotional intensity of their work. However, this detachment can inadvertently compromise the therapeutic relationship and hinder the effectiveness of therapy. Clients may sense the lack of genuine connection or perceive the clinician as aloof, leading to a breakdown in trust and reduced engagement in the therapeutic process.

- **Depersonalization** is a detached and cynical attitude toward clients or the therapeutic process, in which clients are often perceived as objects or cases rather than individuals with unique needs and experiences. As a clinician becomes increasingly detached and disconnected from their clients, they may experience a decline in job satisfaction and a sense of professional disillusionment. The lack of emotional connection and fulfillment in their work can further contribute to emotional exhaustion and erode their overall well-being.

- **Reduced personal accomplishment** refers to the decline in the therapist's perceived competence and effectiveness. They may question their skills, their expertise, and the impact of their interventions—sometimes even questioning the meaningfulness of their work. The sense of fulfillment and purpose that once drove their dedication to helping others may fade away, and they may reach a point where they feel like they don't make a difference to anyone, they don't see the point of their profession, or they are having thoughts of self-harm or suicide.

The potential for clinician burnout escalates when you have clients that present with more severe issues, when you have gone through personal trauma, when you are carrying a high caseload, and when you experience difficulties with coworkers or employers (Yang & Hayes, 2020; O'Connor et al., 2018). The reality is that clinicians often face demanding caseloads, tight schedules, and administrative responsibilities, leaving little time for self-care and relaxation. The sheer volume of clients and the intensity of the work can be emotionally and physically draining. This is not to mention that many clinicians struggle with insufficient resources, have limited access to supervision or consultation, do not receive adequate training, and lack organizational support. Clinicians who struggle with perfectionism, high self-expectations, poor boundaries, and self-care are at higher risk of burnout, too, as are those who tend to engage in excessive self-sacrifice or use ineffective stress-management strategies.

The following are all indicators that you may be experiencing burnout:

- You don't feel like you make a difference anymore.

- None of your clients are making progress.

- You believe most people are out for themselves.

- You think that you aren't getting paid what you are worth and that this will never change.

- You fantasize about running away.

- You believe most people have bad intentions.

- You can't stand going to work. Sometimes it makes you feel sick.

- You haven't had a vacation in a long time.

- You think you can't take time off because your clients need you.

- You feel like you don't have any control over your life circumstances.

- You've been told that you have a bad attitude or are negative.

- You have sabotaged your relationships.

- You have suicidal thoughts.

- You are drinking more or have started using drugs.

- You have relapsed in your recovery program.

Addressing Vicarious Trauma and Burnout

Although vicarious trauma and burnout can interfere with your personal and professional life when left untreated, several factors can help prevent you from reaching this point. This includes engaging in regular self-care practices, seeking adequate social support from supervisors and peers (along with having a sense of autonomy at work and a clear sense of your role and value), having a balanced and diverse caseload, and attending therapy (Sutton et al., 2022).

Practice Self-Care

As you read earlier in this book, self-care is essential to well-being. Therefore, just as your clients must take care of themselves, you must also make the time to replenish your mind and body. Although it can be tempting to power through the workday without taking a break—perhaps you even feel like you owe it to your clients to do so—this will only leave you feeling more depleted and less available to your clients. Start by identifying small pockets of time throughout the day that you can dedicate to self-care. It could be as simple as taking short breaks between sessions to engage in deep-breathing exercises, stretching, or practicing mindfulness. Making intentional use of these small moments can help you recharge and reset throughout the day.

Here are some specific ways to incorporate self-care into your daily routine:

- Set clear boundaries between your personal and professional lives. Schedule regular breaks, time off, and vacations to rest and recharge. Avoid overextending yourself and learn to say no when necessary.

- Engage in regular clinical supervision or consultation with peers or mentors. Connecting with other clinicians allows you to reflect on challenging cases, gain insights, and receive emotional support. Joining professional networks or support groups can also foster connections and camaraderie.

- Prioritize your physical well-being by making time for regular physical exercise, such as walking, jogging, yoga, or dancing. Maintain a balanced and nutritious diet, stay hydrated, and get enough sleep. As you know, physical well-being is closely tied to mental and emotional well-being.

- Incorporate mindfulness practices, such as deep-breathing exercises, meditation, or guided imagery, into your daily routine. These techniques can help reduce stress, increase self-awareness, and promote emotional balance.

- Make time for activities that bring you joy and relaxation outside of work. Engage in hobbies, pursue creative outlets, spend time in nature, or indulge in activities that help you unwind and rejuvenate.

- Incorporate short breaks throughout your workday to rest and recharge. End your therapy sessions at 45 to 50 minutes. Engage in brief relaxation exercises, stretch, or take a few minutes to breathe deeply and reset your focus.

- Stay socially connected by maintaining healthy relationships with family, friends, and loved ones. Make time for social activities and engage in meaningful conversations. Having a support network can provide emotional support and a sense of belonging.

- Regularly engage in self-reflection to track your emotional well-being, triggers, and personal growth.

Remember that self-care is not a luxury but a necessity for mental health professionals. By prioritizing your well-being, you can sustain your passion for helping others and create a healthy, balanced work-life integration.

Seek Supervision and Peer Consultation

Supervision and peer consultation play a vital role in your professional development when you are working with victims of gaslighting and narcissistic abuse. The nature of this therapeutic work can be emotionally demanding, challenging, and complex. You may feel overwhelmed and frustrated when progress is slow or when you're faced with significant therapeutic process challenges, such as a client who continually defends the gaslighter's behavior. You may also exhibit countertransference when working with clients who have experienced gaslighting. For example, you might become critical toward an older female client due to the anger you harbor toward your mother. You may also respond to a client in an overprotective manner due to the guilt and shame you feel about not being able to protect your siblings from abuse. Supervision provides a structured and supportive space where you can explore any reactions or countertransference you may be experiencing, develop greater self-awareness, and ensure that you are adhering to ethical guidelines and best practices in trauma-informed care.

Peer consultation complements supervision by giving you an opportunity collaborate with colleagues with similar professional experiences. When treating clients who have experienced emotional abuse, it is important to be able to share cases, discuss challenges, and seek input from others who understand the complexities of this work. If you are feeling stuck with client's progress, consulting with your peers can help you discover new solutions and therapeutic techniques. You may also feel relief and validation when your colleagues discuss experiencing the same challenges.

Furthermore, supervision and peer consultation can help you identify and address potential issues or biases when working with victims of gaslighting. For example, you may have unresolved issues related to past abuse you experienced that cause you to avoid addressing pertinent topics during sessions. You may also experience feelings of anger and frustration because you don't understand why your client "tolerates" mistreatment. Supervision and peer consultation can encourage you to critically examine your assumptions, cultural perspectives, and personal values, deepening your understanding of trauma dynamics and allowing you to refine your interventions to better serve clients from diverse backgrounds.

Maintain a Balanced and Diverse Caseload

Having a balanced and diverse caseload is crucial for your work as a mental health professional, as it allows you to broaden your clinical skills and expertise, assume a versatile and adaptable approach to therapy, develop competence in working with a wide range of human experiences and social contexts, and provide comprehensive and effective care to a broad range of clients. A balanced caseload also mitigates the risk of burnout and compassion fatigue, which is critical when working with victims of gaslighting. As discussed earlier, working exclusively with this population can be emotionally draining, which increases the likelihood of vicarious trauma. By diversifying your caseload, you can balance the emotional demands of your work.

What constitutes a balanced caseload depends on the individual. You may find that you can see up to three clients a week with a history of gaslighting abuse, or you may feel comfortable with a majority of your clients having experienced gaslighting. There is no right or wrong answer to how you balance your caseload. It is about doing what feels comfortable to you and doesn't negatively impact your mental health.

Attend Therapy

Although clinicians are trained professionals with the knowledge and skills to help others, they are not immune to their own emotional and psychological challenges. This is especially the case for clinicians who specialize in gaslighting and narcissistic abuse, as exposure to clients' traumatic experiences may trigger unresolved personal issues and increase emotional strain. Remember that, in this line of work, you will frequently hear and witness accounts of traumatic experiences, which can have a cumulative emotional toll.

To provide effective care to your clients, consider attending your own therapy to address any unresolved personal issues or emotional triggers that may arise during your work with clients. For example, perhaps you have been feeling anger when working with clients whose children are witnessing emotional abuse. Or maybe you've been finding it hard to not overly self-disclose when a client's story is remarkably similar to yours. You may be experiencing dissociation when your client discusses a particular event. Regardless, therapy of your own is a place where you can work through any countertransference or vicarious trauma you may be experiencing, enabling you to process your emotions and prevent burnout. Consider teletherapy if you are wary of seeing a therapist in your local area. It is essential, and a requirement of your licensure, to seek help when needed. Otherwise, you run the risk of professional and personal liability.

Conclusion

In this workbook, you have delved into the complex dynamics of gaslighting and its profound impact on its victims. As a clinician, you play a crucial role in supporting and empowering clients who have experienced this type of abuse. Your dedication to helping them heal and reclaim their sense of self is admirable.

Remember, treating victims of gaslighting requires compassion, empathy, and a trauma-informed approach. Continue to educate yourself on the intricacies of gaslighting and its associated psychological effects. Stay attuned to your self-care needs as you sit with clients' distress, empathize with their pain, and support them through challenging situations.

Remember, too, that each client's path toward healing is unique, and progress may come in small steps. Be patient, compassionate, and nonjudgmental as you guide them through this process. Trust in your skills and the therapeutic relationship you build with your clients.

As you embark on this journey, I wish you strength, resilience, and the ability to create a safe and validating therapeutic space. Your role as a clinician can be transformative, providing victims the support they need to heal and regain control over their lives. May you find fulfillment and satisfaction in this work as you continue to support and empower those affected by gaslighting.

References

Adkins, K. C. (2019). Gaslighting by crowd. *Social Philosophy Today*, *35*, 75–87. https://doi.org/10.5840/socphiltoday201971660

Ahern, K. (2018). Institutional betrayal and gaslighting: Why whistle-blowers are so traumatized. *The Journal of Perinatal & Neonatal Nursing*, *32*(1), 59–65. https://doi.org/10.1097/JPN.0000000000000306

Allbaugh, L. J., Mack, S. A., Culmone, H. D., Hosey, A. M., Dunn, S. E., & Kaslow, N. J. (2018). Relational factors critical in the link between childhood emotional abuse and suicidal ideation. *Psychological Services*, *15*(3), 298–304. https://doi.org/10.1037/ser0000214

American Psychiatric Association. (2022). *Diagnostic and statistical manual of mental disorders* (5th ed., text rev.). https://doi.org/10.1176/appi.books.9780890425787

Bandelow, B., & Wedekind, D. (2015). Possible role of a dysregulation of the endogenous opioid system in antisocial personality disorder. *Human Psychopharmacology: Clinical and Experimental*, *30*(6), 393–415. https://doi.org/10.1002/hup.2497

Boroujerdi, F. G., Kimiaee, S. A., Yazdi, S. A. A., & Safa, M. (2019). Attachment style and history of childhood abuse in suicide attempters. *Psychiatry Research*, *271*, 1–7. https://doi.org/10.1016/j.psychres.2018.11.006

Brewin, C. R. (2020). Complex post-traumatic stress disorder: A new diagnosis in ICD-11. *BJPsych Advances*, *26*(3), 145–152. https://doi.org/10.1192/bja.2019.48

D'Arienzo, M. C., Boursier, V., & Griffiths, M. D. (2019). Addiction to social media and attachment styles: A systematic literature review. *International Journal of Mental Health and Addiction*, *17*(4), 1094–1118. https://doi.org/10.1007/s11469-019-00082-5

Effiong, J. E., Ibeagha, P. N., & Iorfa, S. K. (2022). Traumatic bonding in victims of intimate partner violence is intensified via empathy. *Journal of Social and Personal Relationships*, *39*(12), 3619–3637. https://doi.org/10.1177/02654075221106237

Green, A., MacLean, R., & Charles, K. (2020). Unmasking gender differences in narcissism within intimate partner violence. *Personality and Individual Differences*, *167*, Article 110247. https://doi.org/10.1016/j.paid.2020.110247

Heshmati, R., Zemestani, M., & Vujanovic, A. (2022). Associations of childhood maltreatment and attachment styles with romantic breakup grief severity: The role of emotional suppression. *Journal of Interpersonal Violence*, *37*(13–14), NP11883–NP11904. https://doi.org/10.1177/0886260521997438

Holland, J. L. (1997). *Making vocational choices: A theory of vocational personalities and work environments* (3rd ed.). Psychological Assessment Resources.

Horowitz, L. M., Bridge, J. A., Teach, S. J., Ballard, E., Klima, J., Rosenstein, D. L., Wharff, E. A., Ginnis, K., Cannon, E., Joshi, P., & Pao, M. (2012). Ask Suicide-Screening Questions (ASQ): A brief instrument for the pediatric emergency department. *Archives of Pediatrics & Adolescent Medicine*, *166*(12), 1170–1176. https://doi.org/10.1001/archpediatrics.2012.1276

Horowitz, L. M., Snyder, D. J., Boudreaux, E. D., He, J.-P., Harrington, C. J., Cai, J., Claassen, C. A., Salhany, J. E., Dao, T., Chaves, J. F., Jobes, D. A., Merikangas, K. R., Bridge, J. A., & Pao, M. (2020). Validation of the Ask Suicide-Screening Questions for adult medical inpatients: A brief tool for all ages. *Psychosomatics, 61*(6), 713–722. https://doi.org/10.1016/j.psym.2020.04.008

Karakurt, G., & Silver, K. E. (2013). Emotional abuse in intimate relationships: The role of gender and age. *Violence and Victims, 28*(5), 804–821. https://doi.org/10.1891/0886-6708.VV-D-12-00041

Kroenke, K., & Spitzer, R. L. (2002). The PHQ-9: A new depression diagnostic and severity measure. *Psychiatric Annals, 32*(9), 509–515. https://doi.org/10.3928/0048-5713-20020901-06

Minuchin, S. (1974). *Families and family therapy.* Harvard University Press.

Nakagawa, T., Koan, I., Chen, C., Matsubara, T., Hagiwara, K., Lei, H., Hirotsu, M., Yamagata, H., & Nakagawa, S. (2020). Regular moderate- to vigorous-intensity physical activity rather than walking is associated with enhanced cognitive functions and mental health in young adults. *International Journal of Environmental Research and Public Health, 17*(2), Article 614. https://doi.org/10.3390/ijerph17020614

O'Connor, K., Neff, D. M., & Pitman, S. (2018). Burnout in mental health professionals: A systematic review and meta-analysis of prevalence and determinants. *European Psychiatry, 53,* 74–99. https://doi.org/10.1016/j.eurpsy.2018.06.003

Pooley, K., & Boxall, H. (2020). Mobile dating applications and sexual and violent offending. *Trends and Issues in Crime and Criminal Justice, 612,* 1–16. https://doi.org/10.52922/ti04862

Posner, K., Brown, G. K., Stanley, B., Brent, D. A., Yeshiva, K. V., Oquendo, M. A., Currier, G. W., Melvin, G. A., Greenhill, L., Shen, S., & Mann, J. J. (2011). The Columbia Suicide Severity Rating Scale: Initial validity and internal consistency findings from three multisite studies with adolescents and adults. *American Journal of Psychiatry, 168*(12), 1266–1277. https://doi.org/10.1176/appi.ajp.2011.10111704

Smyth, J. M., Johnson, J. A., Auer, B. J., Lehman, E., Talamo, G., & Sciamanna, C. N. (2018). Online positive affect journaling in the improvement of mental distress and well-being in general medical patients with elevated anxiety symptoms: A preliminary randomized controlled trial. *JMIR Mental Health, 5*(4), Article e11290. https://doi.org/10.2196/11290

Strathearn, L., Giannotti, M., Mills, R., Kisely, S., Najman, J., & Abajobir, A. (2020). Long-term cognitive, psychological, and health outcomes associated with child abuse and neglect. *Pediatrics, 146*(4), Article e20200438. https://doi.org/10.1542/peds.2020-0438

Sutton, L., Rowe, S., Hammerton, G., & Billings, J. (2022). The contribution of organisational factors to vicarious trauma in mental health professionals: A systematic review and narrative synthesis. *European Journal of Psychotraumatology, 13*(1), Article 2022278. https://doi.org/10.1080/20008198.2021.2022278

Valentine, J. L., Miles, L. W., Mella Hamblin, K., & Worthen Gibbons, A. (2022). Dating app facilitated sexual assault: A retrospective review of sexual assault medical forensic examination charts. *Journal of Interpersonal Violence.* https://doi.org/10.1177/08862605221130390

World Health Organization. (2022). *ICD-11: International classification of diseases* (11th revision). https://icd.who.int/

Yang, Y., & Hayes, J. A. (2020). Causes and consequences of burnout among mental health professionals: A practice-oriented review of recent empirical literature. *Psychotherapy, 57*(3), 426–436. https://doi.org/10.1037/pst0000317

About the Author

Stephanie Moulton Sarkis, PhD, NCC, DCMHS, LMHC, is a renowned therapist and leading expert on gaslighting. With over two decades of experience as a clinician, author, and speaker, Dr. Sarkis has become a trusted voice in the fight against gaslighting and related forms of psychological manipulation. She is the author of seven books and two workbooks. Her groundbreaking book *Gaslighting: Recognize Manipulative and Emotionally Abusive People—and Break Free* has become a must-read for anyone seeking to understand the devastating impact of gaslighting and how to heal from its effects. Her follow-up book, *Healing from Toxic Relationships: 10 Essential Steps to Recover from Gaslighting, Narcissism, and Emotional Abuse*, has also earned critical acclaim.

Dr. Sarkis was named a Diplomate and Clinical Mental Health Specialist in Child and Adolescent Counseling by the American Mental Health Counselors Association, one of only 20 professionals in the United States with this dual designation. She is also a National Certified Counselor, Licensed Mental Health Counselor, and Florida Supreme Court Certified Family and Circuit Mediator. She has been in private practice for over 20 years. Dr. Sarkis earned a PhD, EdS, and MEd in Mental Health Counseling from the University of Florida, named by *U.S. News and World Report* as the top counselor education program in the country. She has taught the graduate-level classes Diagnosis and Assessment of Mental Health Disorders and Law and Ethics of Counseling at the University of Florida and Florida Atlantic University.

Dr. Sarkis is a senior contributor for *Forbes* online and a contributor to *Psychology Today*, where her posts have been viewed over 70 million times. Her *Psychology Today* article "11 Red Flags of Gaslighting in a Relationship" went viral, with over 15 million views. Dr. Sarkis has appeared on CNN, *Ten Percent Happier with Dan Harris*, Sirius XM Doctor Radio, ABC (US), and ABC (Australia), and she has been published in *USA Today*, *The Washington Post*, *Newsweek*, and many more media outlets. Her research on comorbid ADHD and its impact on pediatric executive function was published in the *Journal of Attention Disorders*. She hosts the *Talking Brains* podcast and is based in Tampa, Florida. Visit her at www.stephaniesarkis.com.